Theological Language

ANTONIO ROSMINI

THEOLOGICAL LANGUAGE

Translated by
DENIS CLEARY

ROSMINI HOUSE
DURHAM

©2004 T.P.Watson

Rosmini House, Woodbine Road
Durham DH1 5DR, U.K.

Website: www.rosmini-in-english.org

Translated from
Il Linguaggio Teologico
Città Nuova Edition, vol. 38, Rome, 1975

Unless otherwise noted, the Sscripture quotations contained herein
are from the Revised Standard Version Bible,
copyright 1946, 1952, 1971
by the Division of Christian Education
of the National Council of the Churches of Christ
in the United States of America,
and are used with permission

Typeset by Rosmini House, Durham
Printed by Bell & Bain Limited, Glasgow

ISBN 1 899093 01 X

Note

The many and long quotations in Latin used by the author have been translated. An *asterisk* indicates that the original Latin can be found in the section entitled 'Original Latin References' at the rear of the book (p. 60).

Square brackets [ ] indicate notes or additions by the translator.

Foreword

This booklet is the first theological work of Rosmini to be translated into English but is not entirely alien to the series of translations of his philosophical works carried out over these last eighteen years. He had in mind, for the complete 'Collection' of his works, a section entitled 'The philosophy of supernatural things'. He wanted to construct a philosophy which, following a very genuine and critical process of rational investigation, could serve as a foundation for religious truth. The right order to follow in this study was first reason (philosophy) and then the content of revelation (theology). This explains the many philosophical works he wrote and published and why his theological works were fewer and nearly all incomplete and left in manuscript form. He intended to add *Theological Language* to his moral works to serve as an introduction to this theological section of his plan.

But, apart from its theological importance, the work has importance for any philosophical treatise because the use of words is a perennial problem in human discussion and Rosmini was as fully aware of this as any author. From his earliest years he had dedicated himself to the search for truth and called what he wrote 'the system of truth'. This search for and fidelity to truth demanded much profound and arduous reflection, scrupulous analysis of ideas and deep penetration into the mysteries of nature and life. But of course none of his discoveries and teachings could be communicated to others except through language, above all, written language. Hence, the paramount importance of the precision and discipline of this communication. He saw that it would be a betrayal to omit problems and concepts demanding solid concentration simply because the concepts might cause difficulty in comprehension; the search for truth must be determined and far-reaching, not limited, narrow and superficial. His awareness of this importance of language and the use of words is apparent in nearly all his works. He continually insists that the meaning of words must not be changed, otherwise all discussion is profitless and the search for truth is compromised. For him, the meaning of words was always the meaning given by people in general, by common speech, and this is the meaning that any serious author will want to convey as he writes. It was precisely this lack of the correct understanding and use of words, this re-interpretation and change of their meaning, that compelled him to compose the present work.

This problem of language became more acute when the subject was theological because here one was dealing with revealed truths, truths not verifiable by the senses but demanding faith. But since the time of the Christian revelation, there were those who had meditated deeply on revealed truths and in doing so had come to know more of the truth. St. Augustine, a prolific writer, was aware of this problem of language and wrote to defend its use in expounding and enriching doctrine. But he was attacked for his so-called newness of language and misuse of words, and these attacks did not end with his death. They continued on through the centuries. In the 18th century, the Italian scholar, L.A.Muratori (1672-1750), writing under the pseudonym of Lamindo Pritanio, wrote an answer to the latest attack on Augustine. Muratori himself was writing on textual criticism and reform but, like others, did not escape the opposition of those who failed to understand the language used to develop teaching and deepen knowledge of truth.

For Rosmini, the problem and the unfortunate results it could cause began with the publication (in 1839) of his work 'Conscience'. In this work, he dedicated a chapter to deliberate and indeliberate morality, where he distinguishes between *sin* and *fault*. Sin is present when the will departs from the rectitude of the law, although the will may not be acting freely; *fault* is present when the will acts evilly but with freedom of choice. This distinction could not be discussed without reference to the Catholic teaching on original sin, and it was here that theologians, writing mainly anonymously, took him to task. Rosmini vigorously defended his teaching, but battle was now ferociously engaged.

His opponents considered his language dangerous, inappropriate and obscure, because he departed from traditional language and used new expressions without corresponding terms in Scripture, the Fathers and the Magisterium of the Church. He was accused of various heresies. Even some of his supporters found his language contorted and difficult, stilted. But in a letter to a friend he revealed how conscientious he had been in the use of words: 'I have taken all the care I could to avoid inappropriate and ambiguous expressions that might cause suspicion and wrong understanding. I chose expressions which seemed to me more precise, and from which errors could not be extracted. To keep to this purpose, I have never neglected to go through my works from beginning to end when preparing a new edition. I have always added explanations, comparisons and examples wherever I thought it might be helpful or necessary or would clarify better certain scholastic or technical expressions. These expressions, being little known, could either appear new or be misunderstood. Similarly, whenever I have been asked for a clarification, I have not delayed to give it'. As the controversy became more widespread, the Pope of the time, Gregory XVI, imposed silence on both sides, but that did not settle matters. Eventually in 1848, under Gregory's successor, Pius IX, two of Rosmini's works were put on the Index of Forbidden Books, and at the same time the Pope ordered a full examination of all his published works. This was carried out over the following years with a happy ending: in July 1854, a solemn declaration was made by the Holy See dismissing all his writings as free from error.

With his name cleared, he felt he must go to the heart of the matter and clarify how language must be used by authors and how it should be understood by the reader. In October of that year, three months after the papal declaration, he began *Theological Language*. Unfortunately, he never completed it before his death in July 1855. The manuscript lay unpublished until 1880 and even then was not published in its entirety. Only in 1975 did it appear for the first time in its full form, in the Italian critical edition of Rosmini's works (from which this present translation has been made). The critical edition classifies it, fittingly, as the first volume of his theological works and it is the least known of all his published material. The work was to consist of two parts, the first dealing with theological language, the second with the question of original sin, but the second part was never written, and even the first was not completed.

He wrote *Theological Language* to make his thought clearer, more for others than for himself. It can in fact be read as a kind of autobiography of the process of his thought, as he gently introduces the reader into his system. As a work to help our understanding of what another is saying, especially in written works, it is a sober instruction and perennially relevant for anyone seeking truth.

Finally, and sadly, the translator of this work, Denis Cleary, died before the book was ready for the printer. He had left the foreword till last but was unable to write it. I have tried to compose it in accord with his thoughts and intentions.

TERENCE WATSON

Durham,
February, 2004

Contents

PART ONE

The principles of expression according to which Catholic writers should express themselves

INTRODUCTION

Stresa, 29th October, 1854

1. Modern disbelief, the offspring of 16th century Protestantism, first took root in Holland before passing through England to France, which it shook to its foundations. From France it spread throughout Europe. Its immediate aim, sought with indefatigable energy, was the destruction of Catholicism, which would depend in the first place upon the overthrow of Scholastic philosophy, a willing assistant and companion of the theology with which it had come to maturity.

The spirit of disbelief did all it could to divide reason from faith. It purported to show these two guides of mankind at odds with one another, and pretended to use the weapons proper to reason to combat faith. However, because reason and philosophy, if they are to be worthy of these names, cannot be out of step with faith, disbelief could succeed in its aim only by undertaking the destruction of philosophy in the schools through mockery and sophistry. Disbelief intended to deprive philosophy of the sublime truths upon which its existence is based, in particular of teaching about God, about the soul, and about the nature of intelligible things, upon which the knowledge of God and of the soul depend.

As a result, mankind was deceived into accepting as philosophy a disorganised mass of material knowledge and fallacious arguments. Disbelief was free to parade before the whole world under the name of philosophy, or philosophers, while only a phantasm of philosophy remained in the schools. Although pure materialism was proposed in vain, unbelievers were happy enough to formulate and synthesise all philosophical knowledge under the headings of sensism and subjectivism. The first of these systems makes truth a human sensation, and the second transforms God himself and the world into creatures of the human spirit. These so-called systems became the arsenals from which weapons were drawn to attack every truth in religion and morals. Souls were savaged in immense numbers because the battle was waged against a disarmed generation incapable of defending itself.

Religion cannot in fact defend itself without solid, truthful philosophy. As Leo X said in the 5th Lateran Council, what is true cannot be opposed to what is true; every objection dependent upon reasoning by the enemies of the faith can be answered by reason only. Wisely, therefore, he encouraged philosophers to combat the errors of their time by setting reasoning against reasoning.

2. The Catholic Church, in her desire to overcome the objections of unbelievers and, with equal urgency, to organise revealed truths and penetrate their understanding, has always protected philosophical study, and stimulated those who cultivate and promote it for the same ends. For this reason, estimable religious men, including the great Cardinal Sigismund Gerdil, undertook the difficult task of restoring sound philosophy from the ruin to which it had sunk under blows inflicted by the enemies of religion when disbelief disguised itself as philosophy. Such restoration has also been my aim in my published works, as I have stated more at length in the introduction to them.

3. The style and method proper to philosophical work was therefore in keeping with the aim and the arguments I had in view. Even the theological subjects treated in passing (it is impossible to prescind from them entirely in a complete system of philosophy) took on a philosophical aspect, and progressed through the analyses, distinctions and arguments proper to philosophical discussion. This, however, gave rise to an awkward and unexpected difficulty on my part.

On the one hand, I found myself encouraged by the support of many learned men, amongst them some holding positions of the highest dignity in the Church, who raised my hope that my religious aim was in part succeeding. On the other hand, some theologians did not sufficiently understand subjects treated in this way, and thought there were serious errors in what I had written. They made this clear to the public in a great number of books, and denounced my works as erroneous to the holy apostolic See. The Pope ordered the Sacred Roman Congregation of the Index to examine the works thoroughly, and a short time ago they were declared free from any solid foundation for accusation.[1] What seemed harmful, God turned to good.

4. Despite the dissipation of grave doubts about the soundness of the teaching, some wise and honourable persons were still hesitant about the possible obscurity of these philosophical works with their new language, and thought it might be of help, at least to less understanding readers, if certain points proper to theology, or common to theology and philosophy, were clarified. No particular proposition or expression was indicated, but general comments were made about the very difficult doctrine on original sin and human freedom where, it seemed, greater clarification and more common theological language could be helpful. It is true that writings gain in understanding in so far as they reach the end intended by their authors, and this is especially the case, even for less learned people, if they leave no doubt whatsoever in the minds of their readers when dealing with delicate and important subjects bordering upon our holy faith.

Out of respect for these opinions, I have decided to introduce this new edition of my moral writings with a study of the suggested obscurity and novelty of language in them, and to attempt to clarify the two points mentioned above in order to satisfy all those who are one with me in loving pure, Catholic teaching, and in desiring what is good.

5. Several ways occur to mind of carrying out this duty, to which charity and love of progress in truth impel me. Perhaps the shortest and most helpful is to divide the study into two parts.

First, I shall set out in general the principles and duties of any writer, but especially of one having to deal with theological matters. Here we shall be concerned with clarity, propriety and consecrated use of language. Because the principles and duties I have in mind are those upon which all writers have to be judged,

[1] [Cf. Foreword, p. viii].

there will be no need to speak about my works in this first part. We shall be examining generalities only.

In the second part, I shall begin by offering a brief synthesis of the teaching I have expressed on freedom and on original sin.[2] I hope that this compendium, set out in clearer words commonly used by Catholic theologians, will provide my kind critics with a satisfactory résumé of the system, and that they will be able to recognise in it the clarifications they desire.

The compendium should serve as a key to an easy understanding of the teaching, developed and sustained more at length elsewhere by philosophical reasoning. After this I shall be able, for the sake of greater clarity, to expound the reasons which forced me to write as I did, leaving matters in apparent obscurity for those whose unfamiliarity with philosophical writers leads them to think that my style and way of reasoning is new.

May God grant that I may entirely remove every shadow of suspicion and doubt from the minds of the learned theologians with whom I am arguing and who, without any other ulterior end, want only what I want. May the effort I make show them my desire not only to profess sound doctrine, but to express it clearly and exactly, as far as I can, so that no faithful Christian may have any doubt about what I think.

[2] [Cf. Foreword, p. vii].

[5]

PART ONE

The principles of expression according to which Catholic writers should express themselves

CHAPTER 1

Obscurity in writing, and its causes

6. Generally speaking, a writer has a duty to express himself clearly. It is not easy, however, to define what constitutes clarity and obscurity in writing, although some kind of criterion for judging obscurity in a writer may be established if we consider the possible causes of obscurity.

Victorinus, a celebrated 4th century orator teaching at Rome, reduced these causes to three. According to him, they depend either upon 'the immensity of the matter in hand, or lack of skill in the teacher, or obtuseness in the reader.'*[3] We can express these three causes of obscurity in a more general way: obscurity depends upon the difficulty of the subject, upon the writer, or upon the reader. We shall study each of these causes briefly, beginning with the obscurity produced by the writer himself.

[3] St. Jerome, *On Ezechiel.*, bk. 13.

CHAPTER 2

Obscurity dependent upon writer or speaker

7. A writer or speaker can express himself obscurely through lack of skill, through negligence or malice, or for some praiseworthy end. If the writer's incapacity embraces his subject-matter as well as his way of expressing himself, he could suitably be reminded of Horace's, 'Writers should choose subjects on a par with their powers; and think carefully of the burdens they are able or not able to embrace.'*[4]

If he knows his material, but expresses himself defectively, the fault may not be too serious. Not everyone can achieve the same kind of skill in expression, and it does occur that profound and learned persons, bereft of the gift of natural, clear and easy diction, cannot make up for it even with great effort. Heraclitus the Obscure, as he was called, is a good example. In some outstanding persons, however, obscurity in expression is the result not of carelessness, but of their exaggerated search for metaphor or simile or brevity: 'In striving to be brief, I become obscure.'*[5]

8. Obscurity arising from negligence is more culpable, especially if it betrays confused concepts rather than neglect in style. Here, the Catholic writer has a very grave duty, when dealing with dogma or morality, to employ great care in ensuring that obscurity does not give rise to equivocal teaching that could reasonably be interpreted in a mistaken sense. This kind of negligence could throw suspicion on the purity of a writer's faith, or seriously harm the faithful in contact with the ambiguity.

Nevertheless, excessive criticism is to be avoided at this point. Not every equivocal expression can be laid to the bad will or the negligence of the writer. Even the best religious writers cannot refrain from occasional verbal ambiguities which are adequately rectified by the general presentation of their teaching. Moreover, the rigorous, competent language required in dealing with abstract and subtle doctrines, especially in theology, cannot be thought out and perfected by one person alone. This comes

[4] [Horace, *Art*, 38–40].

[5] [*Ibid.*, 25–26].

about with time and study, and application to the problem by many learned people. Even now, after so many controversies and so much thought on the part of saints and theologians, it would be out of place to maintain that language has been finally perfected in every respect. A great deal has been achieved, and theological language has been approved in large part by the authority of the Church and common consent amongst theologians, but this has been done gradually as hidden ambiguities have come to light through erroneous interpretations. Even the Fathers of the Church *liberius loquebantur* [spoke more freely], before heresies made them more cautious, as Augustine says.[6] One of the benefits unwillingly rendered by heretics to sacred doctrine and to the Church of Jesus Christ has been to make ecclesiastical writers more wary and exact in the exposition of revealed dogmas. Augustine noted this: 'What is wrong on the part of heretics has helped progress on the part of true Catholic members of Christ. What is wrong, God uses well, and all things work towards the good of those who love God.'*[7]

However, grave malice is present in those writers who disguise perverse teaching in obscurity in order to impress it more easily upon simple people, or to avoid censure by the Church. Heretics, especially the more astute and subtle such as Arians, Jansenists, Pelagians and so on, have provided many well-known examples of such detestable malice. When they were under pressure from defenders of Catholic faith, and still more after their condemnation by the Church, they worked hard to deck out their errors in expressions which were either unclear or in great part Catholic. This made it difficult to uncover and pin-point where they had abandoned Catholic faith and inserted their own error.

Finally, a writer or a speaker can deliberately produce a certain, moderate obscurity in his work without causing ambiguity about matters of belief. This may be praiseworthy rather than defective, if it is done with a good end in view. The Scriptures,

[6] *Against Julian,* 1, n. 22. *Vobis non litigantibus securius loquebatur* [He spoke to you with greater surety before you quarrelled] (St. John Chrysostom).

[7] *City of God,* 18; 51. Cf. *City of God,* 16, 2; *Letter 105*; *On True Religion,* c. 8; *Genesis against the Manichaeans,* I, 1.

for example, sometimes provide such respectable obscurity, destined, as Augustine says, ‘to exercise and temper in some way the minds of readers, to break down the difficulties and focus the efforts of those wishing to learn, and to veil the spirits of the impious so that they either be converted to piety or excluded from the mysteries.’*[8]

This obscurity cannot, however, be imitated by Christian teachers, who are obliged to elucidate the doctrines contained in God’s written word with the greatest possible clarity. Nevertheless, a person sent by JESUS Christ can and must adapt his way of teaching to different types of people, just as the great Master of mankind veiled the superabundant light of doctrine with parables or enigmas, and gradually disclosed the mystery to his disciples as they grew more capable of penetrating it. Sometimes the teacher can usefully omit obscure parts, provided there is no equivocation about truths to be believed, in order to stimulate reflection and arouse a desire for further understanding in the minds of his more eager disciples.

[8] *On Christian Teaching*, 4, 22.

CHAPTER 3

Obscurity dependent upon reader or hearer

9. However clear a writer may be, his work may still be obscure for some of his readers. Here we are dealing with what is commonly called 'relative obscurity', found in the mind or on the lips of readers rather than in the written work itself. In the mind, it depends upon lack of understanding caused by insufficient intelligence or insufficient knowledge. When simply stated, but when not actually present in the mind, it depends on pretending not to understand, or pretending to misunderstand. If found guilty of false interpretation, these readers unjustly accuse the author of obscurity in order to excuse the calumny they have brought against him. Incapacity, therefore, and malice cause readers to find or to call obscure what has been written with perfect clarity. The two elements are often mixed in varying proportions.

10. As we said, readers' incapacity may depend upon lack of intelligence or lack of knowledge. Books treating a branch of knowledge totally unknown to a reader are bound to be obscure for him. Mathematics, for example, is the clearest of all sciences, but books on it are invariably obscure for people who have never studied the subject. The same can be said about books on physics in the hands of those unfamiliar with the principles of physics, or about philosophy books, and about any other scientific discipline. This kind of relative obscurity arises from lack of requisite knowledge for understanding the works. The writer has fully satisfied his obligation to be clear when what he has written is expressed clearly in itself, and relatively to the class of readers for whom he writes and for whom his book is of its nature intended. A reader unfamiliar with the subject of the book may judge absolutely that it is obscure, but that is indicative of presumption and temerity on his part. His opinion does not bring disrepute on the writer. The same can be said when a writer is accused of obscurity by someone who, although incapable of understanding what has been written clearly, nevertheless passes judgment on the work. Just as the

writer has to measure his own forces before undertaking some scientific argument, every reader has an equal duty to weigh carefully his own capacity before judging the clarity or obscurity of any book: *Caecus non iudicat de colore* [A blind person does not judge colour].

11. Readers sin much more seriously, however, if they are prevented from understanding by blind passion, or pretend not to understand, or misunderstand through malice aforethought, whether their bad will is directed towards the writer or the written truth. This is the case with all those who cling obstinately to their own opinions, or are motivated by some secret interest. Heretics who express misunderstanding of the Church's teaching and oppose it with maxims and dogmas invented by themselves are supreme examples of this.

12. St. Augustine himself was often accused of obscurity, despite his genius, his eloquence, his wisdom and the great love which impelled him to speak to all the faithful as clearly as the level of argument permitted. His sacrifice of classical Latin,[9] and his continual prayer for grace[10] to make himself clear to the faithful, did not absolve him in the sight of his opponents. But he was deeply humble, and in his Retractions[11] would have sincerely acknowledged any conscious defect of obscurity. True humility is incapable of deceit or lies; and it was the firm persuasion of truth which conquered in him when he defended himself vigorously against an accusation that could have harmed the holy cause he sustained against the heretics. With the frankness that normally accompanies sincere humility, he begged his adversaries not to calumniate him with accusations of obscurity, but pray to God for the grace to understand what he had

[9] Cf. *On Christian Teaching*, bk. 4, c. 10, where he shows that in teaching uneducated people religious truths, catechists have to know how to abandon pure, elegant speech for the sake of making themselves understood.

[10] There are innumerable places in his works, and even in his sermons to the people, when he begs God not only to enlighten him but also give him words which his hearers can understand. And he prays also that his hearers may have the light to understand.

[11] We are speaking of theological matters. The holy Doctor says that some of his first philosophical writings depended more on his own lack of formation and on his obscurity than on his will. Cf. the book, *On the Immortality of the Soul*, in *Retractions,* 1, c. 5.

written clearly: 'Some still do not understand what I think has been said sufficiently clearly. I beg them not to blame me for negligence or lack of capacity. Rather, let them ask God for enlightenment.'*[12] When Julian, Bishop of Eclanum and defender of the Pelagians, tried to convince people that Augustine's writings were unintelligible, the saint replied: 'People do understand me, whether you like it or not. But you have nothing to say against these things. You want not to understand what I have said, although it is most true and solid.'*[13]

[12] *On the Merits and Forgiveness of Sins and on Infant Baptism*, 3, c. 2.

[13] *Incomplete Work against Julian,* 3, c. 61.

CHAPTER 4

Obscurity arising from difficulties with the subject

13. The third cause of obscurity in written work, according to Victorinus, is the difficulty and immensity of the subject: *ex rei magnitudine*. When a book contains clear ideas presented in exact language, its author and the book itself are not truly obscure, despite difficulty on the part of an unprepared or malicious reader. On the other hand, the book may be obscure because of the difficulty and sublimity of its subject, without fault on the part of the writer. The work may be written clearly from the point of view of ordered material, logical reasoning and careful use of terms, yet still remain obscure from the point of view of content, which the author has endeavoured to clarify.

Nevertheless, a distinction must be made between the *difficulty* of a subject and its obscurity. The former gives rise to obscurity, but only relatively to less able intelligences. This is not absolute, true obscurity, which is found in the subject-matter itself only when no human intelligence can ever fully resolve and remove it.

14. *Difficulty*, but not always obscurity, is found in many problems dealing with the nature of corporeal and spiritual beings. Everyone knows that studies in physics, mathematics and metaphysics present immense difficulties to the human mind. It would be foolish and barbarous, however, to want to ban the study of these subjects because of their difficulty, or to eliminate them from ordinary life on the pretext that they are as dark and obscure as the minds considering them. Civilisation and human society have been able to make progress only through the labours of those subjecting themselves to the work entailed in studies of this kind. The natural instinct of human intelligence stimulates people to bring greater pressure to bear where there are greater difficulties to overcome. Once conquered, difficulties often reveal a precious source of hidden teaching. Moreover St. Augustine rightly observes that 'what is sought with difficulty is sweeter when found.'*[14]

[14] *Exposition on Psalm 103, serm. 2, n. 1.*

15. Are we confronted with intrinsic obscurity in the natural sciences, or only with difficulties? It is not altogether easy to reply to this question. What has often seemed exceptionally hard and insoluble has been overcome with time and perseverance, and the results themselves have presented various degrees of difficulty. Unsolved, the problems may have seemed totally obscure, but their solution has dissipated the obscurity and given rise to lesser obstacles to understanding. Generally speaking, therefore, it has to be said that the natural questions human intelligence can solve are indeed difficult, but only relatively obscure for mankind. They possess no intrinsic obscurity in our regard. The same may be said about true solutions to the same problems: although they may still present difficulties, they are not as a result obscure. It is true that insoluble enigmas may remain in the order of nature. As the Bible says: 'God has made everything suitable for its time; moreover he has put a sense of past and future into their minds, yet they cannot find out what God has done from the beginning to the end.'*[15] But this is the only source of the real obscurity of these subjects, constituting as it does the foundation and base of all human knowledge.

True, intrinsic obscurity in the content of human enquiry is much more dense in the depths of the revealed truths of our faith, which is full of profound mysteries. For this reason, knowledge of these truths outweighs other knowledge in dignity and worth, 'because this branch of knowledge is principally about matters which by reason of their height transcend reason,' as St. Thomas observes,*[16] in words indicating the source of the precious, intrinsic obscurity of faith.

16. However, although we now behold divine matters *per speculum et aenigmate* [in a mirror, dimly], as long as we remain in the present life, we do see something of them. Faith does not propose total darkness for our belief, but light and darkness together. The dark, obscure part of faith can gradually be diminished on our side by the divine light we obtain through prayer and by unceasing meditation. At the same time, we can open our eyes and focus them better on the luminous aspect,

[15] Eccles 3: 11.

[16] *S.T.*, I, 1, 5.

although the veil can never be totally removed. This is the wise plan, God's economy, according to which man has been instructed about the things necessary for eternal bliss. St. Augustine thus expresses the same concept: 'The height of the word of God calls us to work hard; it does not denigrate our understanding. If all were closed, there would be nothing obscure to be revealed. Again, if all were covered, the soul would be without nourishment and without strength with which to knock at what is closed.'*[17]

The dark side of revealed wisdom is proper to faith, the luminous aspect to understanding. I have dealt elsewhere with the order in which these two paths of the human mind progress (*Theodicy*, Book 1, Introduction). Here, I wish to note that what is mysterious and dark in holy doctrine does not prevent the possibility and the necessity of searching within it, with humility and piety, for the light of understanding. Whatever we succeed in grasping, much or little though it may be, is the most precious part of human knowledge. As Aristotle says, 'the least we acquire in knowledge about the highest things is more desirable than the knowledge we hold with unshakeable certainty about lower matters.'[18]

17. The truths contained in the deposit of faith were, therefore, the object of constant meditation and unceasing study in the Church, especially by holy bishops in her early days. They responded to the Apostle's command to Timothy: 'Take heed to yourself and to your teaching; attend to the public reading of scripture, to preaching, to teaching.'*[19] The need to reply to heretics also obliged shepherds and teachers of the flock to use their intellectual powers to penetrate the truths of faith, to express them more explicitly and distinctly, and to order and harmonise them. Their conscientious work reflected the truth of JESUS' words, 'Every scribe who has been trained for the kingdom of heaven brings out of his treasure what is new and what is old.' In this way the truths of faith were enriched, as time passed, through the efforts of holy and learned men, and above all through the dogmatic decisions of the Church. These

[17] *On the Words of the Apostle*, serm. 13, n. 1.

[18] *On the Parts of Animals*, 1, 9.

[19] 1 Tim 4: 16; *ibid.*, 13.

[17]

truths, as they took on unity in design, order and method, came to form the branch of knowledge known as sacred theology.

18. Consentius, who had written to St. Augustine persuaded that *veritatem ex fide magis quam ex ratione percipi oportere* [truth should be perceived through faith rather than reason], nevertheless asked him in the same letter to use the light of his great mind to unfold to him the teaching on the Trinity. In his reply,[20] St. Augustine showed that his request, although not unreasonable, was not in keeping with what Consentius had first said in his letter. Rather, his first opinion, which detracted too much from reason, needed to be modified: 'First, see if what you ask harmonises with your previous definition.'*[21] 'If I am to do what you want,' he declares, 'and help you to penetrate the mystery as far as possible, I have to do so by following reason itself. Nor when I have brought you a little into the understanding of such a secret (which I cannot do in any way without inner help from God) will I be doing anything other than reasoning, as far as I can.'*[22] With these words Augustine shows Consentius how to modify his opinion which attributed everything to authority alone, while retaining authority and at the same time trying to penetrate truths believed unshakeably on the authority of God who reveals. 'So if you, not unreasonably, ask me or any other teacher how to understand what you believe, correct your definition not for the sake of rejecting faith but in order also to behold with the light of reason what you already hold with solid faith.'*[23]

St. Augustine goes on to show that, with faith presupposed as an inescapable and immobile foundation, it is highly praiseworthy to apply the faculty of reason, and natural reasoning itself, to revealed dogmas in order to draw from them greater light for the understanding. God is very pleased with this: 'It cannot be that God hates in us the very thing by which he has made us more excellent than other living beings. It cannot be, I say, that we believe in such a way that we neither accept nor seek what is

[20] *Letter 120*, n. 2.

[21] *Letter 120*.

[22] [*Letter 120*].

[23] [*Ibid.*].

rational. We could not even believe unless we had rational souls.'*[24]

After explaining the intimate relationships that bind reason and faith, and the rules to be followed in the use of both, he distinguishes true reason from false, that is, from that which is not reason at all. He then declares that the person who not only believes, but understands with true reason what he believes, is in a better position than one who believes without understanding, although he desires to understand. If, in fact, he did not desire to understand, he would not even know the purpose of faith. Its final aim is vision, that is, perfect intelligence. 'Again, the person who understands truly what previously he only believed is in a better position than the one who still desires to understand what he believes. But if he does not even desire to understand, and thinks that what is to be understood is only to be believed, he is unaware how faith is of assistance in this matter. Pious faith does not wish to be bereft of hope and charity. The faithful believer, therefore, must believe what he does not yet see in such a way that he may hope and love the vision.'*[25]

He also says that here on earth certain souls must be content with faith alone and with the light which, very precious and extremely helpful, it brings in its wake, while they hope and desire that one day they will understand what they have been promised. But he warmly exhorts others to devote themselves to reflection and thought about God, and about divine, revealed truths, despite their difficulty and profundity.

19. What seems to merit greatest attention, however, is the sign given by Augustine for recognising those who have the capacity for undertaking this kind of study and, by philosophising about God, adding more light, through good use of the speculative mind, to what is taught by authority. The standard is this: their capacity for arriving at an understanding of that which forms pure mind, pure intelligence. Only knowledge of the nature of the mind, an element of our soul, can be applied to the Creator in such a way as to make possible some kind of reasoning about the Being who is above all creation. Those who cannot grasp this doctrine of the mind and intelligence should be

[24] [*Ibid.*].

[25] [*Ibid.*].

content with faith; their souls falter in their own sight, and fail to recognise what is best in themselves, that is, their intellectual element. As Augustine states in setting out with great accuracy the single, true base of Christian philosophy: 'If we consider the soul in this way, that is, especially as human and rational and intellectual, and made according to his image, and we find that it does not overwhelm our thoughts and understanding, but that we are able to grasp with our mind and understanding its foundation, that is, our very mind and understanding, it will not perhaps be absurd for us to contemplate its being brought, with God's help, to the understanding of its Creator. But if the soul is incapable of this, and feels itself falling, let it be satisfied with pious faith as long as it journeys to God. One day that which has been promised will come about in us through him "who by the power at work within us is able to accomplish abundantly far more than all we can ask or imagine".'*[26]

20. There is profound wisdom in this principle according to which Augustine declares that those incapable of forming for themselves a true concept of the nature of the human mind and intelligence are unsuited to rational speculation about divine matters. Careful examination shows that all the errors of philosophers and heretics about God and the Trinity (and some of them were gross indeed) have their origin in their authors' ignorance of the nature of the mind and the intelligence. They formed their concept of it from the likeness to it which they found in things inferior to it; they did not grasp it directly, as it is in itself. And yet they wanted rashly to reason about the things of God.

St. Augustine's teaching takes us even further. He is not content with encouraging us to desire and struggle to reach, as far as humanly possible, through reason combined with prayer, some understanding of the extremely difficult and sublime things that we believe; nor does he think it sufficient to point out the condition on which this can be done, or the principle from which we have to start, that is, an accurate and true theory of the mind and of human knowledge, according to which we are made in the image and likeness of God. He also determines and establishes with great accuracy what is most sublime in our mind and

[26] [*Ibid.*].

intelligence. From this culminating point we can, he says, more securely reach out in thought to God, and come to know him more scientifically.

In our mind and intelligence, the lower part is made up of ourselves who use the mind; the higher, superior part is the *light*, impressed upon us by God himself, by means of which we know and judge all things. This *light* of human reason and intelligence is such that it is not absurd, when we have grasped it, to behold it ascending to God, *ad suum quoque auctorem intelligendum* [to understanding of its Creator]; this is the light continually infused into the human soul by him *qui illuminat omnem hominem venientem in hunc mundum* [who enlightens everyone coming into this world]; this is the starting point for all sound philosophy in its application to divine matters. But we should hear from Augustine himself the magnificent description he gives of this light as a reflection of the divine face. He presents and analyses it in the following way: 'This very light, by which we discern all these things, in which the unknown that we believe is sufficiently clear to us (in so far as it precedes faith), in which we hold what we know, remember the shape of the body that we claim to know, grasp what bodily sense presents us with, imagine how the spirit is like the body, and contemplate with the understanding what is certainly dissimilar to all bodies — this very light, in which all these things are judged, is not diffused through local spaces in the same way as the splendour of our sun and of corporeal light, nor does it enlighten our mind with some kind of visible clarity. Invisibly and ineffably, but nevertheless intelligibly, it shines before us and is as certain to us as all those things which it makes certain to us and which we behold through it.'*[27]

According to Augustine, this light, corresponding to the *principium quo* of the Scholastics, is the source from which man draws all ideas and knowledge;*[28] it is that in which and through which true judgments are formed about all things;*[29] and finally, it contains the principle of certainty, and is itself most certain.*[30]

[27] [*Ibid.*].

[28] [*Ibid.*].

[29] [*Ibid.*].

[30] [*Ibid.*].

St. Augustine wants us to study and investigate the most difficult matters, as far as this is possible; he wants us to make every effort to obtain the greatest possible degree of understanding; but at the same time, he indicates the path we should follow and the principle from which we should start if we do not wish to labour in vain. We have to begin by meditating and understanding the *light* of our intelligence, wherein lies the origin of our ideas and the certainty of our judgments.

[20]

CHAPTER 5
Continuation

21. Human intelligence, therefore, is faced not only with *difficult* matters, but matters which concern many revealed doctrines, both difficult and obscure. No one should imagine himself capable of removing every veil of obscurity in these subjects. He would be aiming for impossible clarity and facility in writing, and any final clarity he gained would be more apparent than real. Nor can a reader demand the impossible from any writer. If works on such subjects contain no error, their remaining obscurity cannot be laid at the door of the author, nor blamed on the book. It simply indicates human limitation in the present life.

22. The obscurity intrinsic to a subject does not oblige a writer to abandon the subject, provided he undertakes to limit its obscurity in every possible way. In natural sciences, honours have been heaped upon those overcoming the difficulties they have encountered; the greatest geniuses, always glad to exercise their talent on more acute difficulties, have never failed to arouse admiration. Holy men and women, and teachers of sacred doctrine, have done the same, and encouraged others with capacity similar to their own to reflect upon the sublime and mysterious truths of religion, in which the greatest difficulty is mixed with the finally unconquerable obscurity proper to such doctrine.

According to St. Thomas, 'Sacred teaching can receive something from philosophical disciplines, not because it needs them, but for the sake of greater clarity about matters handed on in the knowledge of faith.'*[31] This does not depend upon defects or poverty in the teaching nor, as he says, is it a necessary feature of doctrine itself: 'It is demanded by our intellect which is led more easily to things above reason when it sets out with things known to natural reason (reason which gives rise to other branches of knowledge).'*[32]

[31] [*S.T.*, I, q. 1, a. 5, ad 2].

[32] [*Ibid.*, 713].

23. When philosophy is rightly applied to it, the content of sacred doctrine is *illustrated more clearly* according to Aquinas. This is the kind of illumination the Fathers and Doctors of the Church, especially St. Augustine, desired from those whom they encouraged and stimulated in the belief that they were capable of offering it. Such support is useful to piety and to the progress of the kingdom of God on earth, but divine Providence itself placed a new incentive to reflection in the Church when it permitted heretics and God's enemies, or other rash and presumptuous people, to contradict revealed doctrine.

24. Human reasoning has attacked sacred doctrine unceasingly with every kind of subtle, fallacious argument, and provoked the use of contrary weapons based on the finest dialectical expertise. New, opportune distinctions have been needed to define and determine every area of sacred teaching; there should be no room for equivocation concealing deceit and sophistry. And, as St. Augustine often notes,[33] this is one of the great benefits produced by divine wisdom from the evils of heresy and contention. In the 5th Lateran Council also, Pope Leo X encouraged philosophers to solve with reasoning the sophistries brought against the faith by the abuse of reason.

It has always been the Church's desire, therefore, that mankind should attain the greatest possible understanding of the truths believed on the authority of God who reveals, and of the Catholic Church which proposes them. Understood in this way, these truths are subject to greater enlightenment, and rendered immune to attack from the subtle, fallacious arguments of the enemies of the kingdom of God. Unfortunately, our own days have seen the rise of a certain spirit of embarrassment and diffidence in relation to human reason on the part of some devout people. They either want reason totally excluded as incapable of providing mankind with any certainty (leaving the field to faith alone and divine authority); or they take it upon themselves to censure rigorously what they think obscure, whether

[33] *Confessions*, bk. 7, c. 19; *On True Religion*, c. 6–10; *Genesis against the Manichaeans*., 1. c. 1; *Letter 185*, c. 1; *Exposition on Psalm 7*, n. 15; *Ps. 8*, n. 6; *Ps. 9* (other), n. 20; *Ps. 54*, n. 22–24; *Ps. 67*, n. 39; *Ps. 106*, n. 14; *On Faith in Things that are not seen*, c. 7; *On Catechising Beginners*, n. 42–44; *Sermon on the Usefulness of Fasting*, c. 8; *City of God*, bk. 16, c. 2; bk. 18, c. 51; *Against Faustus the Manichee*, 12, c. 24; *On the Gift of Perseverance*, c. 20.

the subject under consideration is truly obscure because of its mystery, or simply difficult, or new to their way of thinking and to the normal path their form of studies has taken.

Some go so far as to maintain that what is difficult is also dangerous; prudence would require its abandonment. If this opinion is understood in its extreme sense, it is directly contrary to the feeling of the whole of antiquity and to human common sense, as well as being an obstacle to the progress of truth and Christian religion itself here on earth. The only thing we can say is that when giving religious instruction to a particular person or group, it is good to restrict oneself to matters proportionate to their capacity for understanding, and to the level of their moral energies. When the listener, or group, possesses a certain culture, higher and more difficult subjects can be discussed. In speaking to the people at large, easier, more elementary subjects should be treated.[34] Even so, St. Augustine, who wanted the Christian teacher to act in this way, was very keen at the same time to stimulate to the limit the intellectual soaring of his faithful, like an eagle with its young. And he was glad to have been able to achieve this often.[35]

25. The situation is different when there is no predetermined audience, as in the case of a writer publishing his work. Naturally, every author has a certain class of persons in mind when he is developing his argument, but he cannot prevent others from reading the book. Readers themselves, therefore, have the duty to take advice and choose the books best suited to their understanding, and most useful for them. A mistaken choice is their fault, not the author's. A mistake will not harm the reader, however, provided he does not undertake the reading rashly and proudly, persuading himself to his own detriment that he

[34] Cf. St. Augustine, *On Christian Teaching*, 4, and *On Catechising Beginners*.

[35] For example, in one of his sermons he speaks to the people as follows: 'In the previous apostolic readings, which I have explained to your charity as far as the Lord in his mercy has enabled me to do, I worked hard and anxiously. I felt with you and was anxious about you. But as I see it, the Lord helped you and me, so that the really difficult passages he vouchsafed to explain through me in such a way that every question dealt with might disturb a pious mind. The impious mind, however, hates understanding'* (*On the Words of the Apostle*, Sermon 13).

understands a work when this is not the case. It is not right that something of this nature should lead to neglect and damage in the cause of truth and of the understanding of what is most sublime and precious for mankind, such as the knowledge of religion. This is the constant teaching of St. Augustine, and what he requires of a person instructing others orally, especially the people, is expressed in the following words: 'There are some things which of their nature are either not understood or barely understood despite the effort made by the speaker. These are to be avoided when the people are present, or mentioned only rarely if needs must.' Authors, however, and those presenting a case to learned men, are to follow another path, as he goes on to say immediately: 'It is different with books, which are written so that they may in some way grip the reader when they are understood or, if they are not understood, are no trouble to the reader (who is under no obligation to read them). Sometimes persistence is needed here, so that the truths we have already penetrated, although very difficult to understand, may lead us with only a little effort to understand other things provided the attention of a capable reader or interlocutor is motivated by the desire to learn. The writer needs to make clear how this understanding is possible. And to do this the teacher should pay more attention to evidence than to eloquence.'*[36]

26. Despite this, devout but over-prudent people can be found advising modern writers to abandon questions too complicated for ordinary intelligences.[37] According to them, teaching of this kind provides no help to religion, and can easily cause dissension and dangerous division when wrongly understood by those incapable of grasping it. Unenlightened zeal is inclined to panic, they say, and take as contrary to faith what is simply a clearer explanation and illustration of the faith itself. Zealous people then attract others amongst the faithful who either fall into uncertainty about the soundness of a writer's doctrine, or condemn it out of hand on the word of the writer's opponents. The result is unrest and disunity among the faithful, to the detriment of charity. But those focusing attention on these deleterious effects see no necessity for asking whether they result from

[36] *On Christian Teaching*, bk 4, c. 9.

[37] [Cf. Foreword, p. vi].

weaknesses inherent in the written word, or from defects in the uncomprehending reader. They show no hesitation, however, about passing judgment, nor in letting their judgment be known.

Such advice is normally withheld until an author has found lively opponents, and given when special circumstances have put him in a position to be criticised. Before blaming the writer, would it not be better to form some opinion about the incalculable value of the truth he illustrates, about the importance of its development in human minds, and finally about the necessity of safeguarding it more effectively against manifest errors and against the germ of error, which is so often detected by such a writer before its growth is perceived by the ordinary faithful? What does the acute, loving and prudent heart of St. Augustine have to say about the matter (his prudence, be it understood, pertains to the realm of the spirit)? In some of his books he had expounded the teaching on grace; no one had thought it new, nor raised any difficulty about it. What was said later, when Pelagians and semi-Pelagians opposed it as though he had introduced something novel into the Church? That Augustine had imprudently stirred up dissension about a difficult question; that he had disturbed simple people by commenting on a question which could have been passed over in silence without loss to any one: 'Certainly, there was no need of this kind of argument which is a source of disturbance to the less intelligent. The Catholic faith was defended for many years, and just as ably, without this definition of predestination.'*[38]

27. St. Augustine was blamed during his own lifetime by the famous Marseillaises, and later by many others, including modern critics who press the charge more strongly. Some have even wondered whether he may not have offered an occasion of eternal damnation to souls.[39] Calumnies of this kind have been

[38] *On the Gift of Perseverance*.

[39] Cf. Luis de Molina in his *Concordia*: 'Augustine's teaching on predestination greatly disturbed many of the faithful, unlearned and learned, especially those in France, and might even have put their salvation in danger'.* Noris, in his *Vindiciae*, offers examples of authors who in the last century attacked Augustine. Many other modern authors fall into the same category.

repeated to the present day despite their constant condemnation by the Church and the popes who, to say the least, have always rejected such an unbalanced charge.

What was St. Augustine's reaction to this criticism? Did it stop him from writing, or bring him to confess humbly (and he was a truly humble man) that he had acted imprudently in dealing with difficult questions, or in writing obscurely? He did neither, but told the faithful for whom he had written that he thought he had expressed himself clearly, and that those who had not understood should ask God for light to comprehend: 'Those who still do not understand what I think I have expressed clearly, granted the nature of the questions, should not calumniate me as though I had been negligent or blame me for my lack of skill. Rather, they should ask God for understanding.'*[40]

Indeed, St. Augustine never tired of explaining the question. He wrote more than thirty works in defence of divine grace, and through them brought many people in good faith with a desire to learn to a greater understanding and love of the truth he was teaching, although the lucidity of his writings was lost on others badly disposed. Amongst the Marseillaises, those who took St. Augustine as an authority, but without understanding his teaching, were enlightened and fully satisfied with his *De correptione et gratia*, written to resolve difficulties brought against his work in Africa. Others found no help in the book, but rather an occasion for greater animosity against its author. St. Prosperus describes the situation in a letter he wrote at the time to St. Augustine: 'Those who have read your Beatitude's book (*De correptione et gratia*) and were already adhering to the holy, apostolic authority of your teaching have understood better and become better informed; the others, who were having difficulty, are more opposed to it than ever.'*[41] St. Augustine added clarification after clarification for the sake of those who 'were having difficulty', but in vain.

28. The difficulties raised by his opponents, but attributed to the saint, persisted for over a century in Gaul after his death, and were revived still later. But truly wise people, and the entire

[40] [*On the Merits and Forgiveness of Sins*, bk. 3, cc. 2, 4].

[41] [Prosper, *Ep*. 1, 2].

Church, were adamant in praising St. Augustine's courage in facing up to blame, calumnies and excessive fear of being misunderstood or causing trouble amongst malicious or badly disposed persons, in his defence and explanation of the truth. In the second half of the 9th century, the church of Lyons and its bishop, St. Remigius, acclaimed Augustine for such courage in its *Book of Three Letters*: 'Nor could his resolution, intent upon the truest and most faithful teaching, be broken or revoked by such perturbation and disturbance amongst the faithful. Rather, he warned and instructed them in his writings, while praying fervently to God for them, so that they might understand and know how necessary and salvific it was that the truth of predestination should be believed and preached to the praise of divine grace.'*[42]

29. Truth is and always has been precious in the eyes of the holy Doctors of the Church. They have always considered work to explain and support it as a great benefit for the faithful and the kingdom of God on earth, and have made light of the opposition aroused by the untutored piety of those incapable of grasping certain difficulties, and by the rashness and malice of others who twist their sense or undermine with sophistries what they had expressed clearly with the best of motives.

[42] c. 35.

CHAPTER 5 [*sic*]

Doctrinal innovation, and innovative ways of unfolding traditional doctrines

30. Efforts are made, therefore, to penetrate the truths of faith with understanding, and illustrate them orally and in writing for the sake of greater knowledge on the part of the faithful who have received from God the ability and the time to learn more. In carrying out this work, the greatest care must be taken to avoid godless innovation, as St. Paul teaches with all the Fathers and Doctors of the Church. The 'deposit' consigned by Christ to the apostles, and handed over by them to their successors (consigned, too, in a special way to the safekeeping of Peter and the bishops of Rome who have succeeded him and will succeed him throughout the ages) cannot be diminished, increased or changed in the slightest. Its divine origin precludes this. The promise of lasting assistance given by Jesus Christ to his Church is a firm guarantee that not even the smallest part of the deposit will be lost. It will be taught in its entirety, and handed on in its entirety, until the second coming of the Redeemer. The teaching, already condemned, which foolishly maintains 'the presence in these last centuries of a general obscurity veiling truths which are the foundation of the faith and of moral teaching'[43] is clearly heretical.

31. But if the deposit of the truths of our holy faith is not susceptible of increase, diminution or change, can we rightly say that it is possible and necessary to meditate, unfold and illustrate them? We must follow the Fathers and Doctors, the best Scholastics, and the soundest of the ecclesiastical writers coming after them. We must do as they have taught. All of them upheld the same unchangeable doctrine of the Church, and through this wonderful harmony of teaching became authoritative witnesses of revealed truths. This is especially true of the Fathers. However, they were not satisfied with attesting and faithfully handing on these truths. Besides acting as witnesses, they undertook the office of teachers. They defended the truths

[43] Bull *Auctorem fidei*, prop. 1.

with abundant arguments; they explained and ordered the truths; they deduced wonderful, inexhaustible consequences implicitly contained in the truths which they compared and co-related when they appeared in contrast with one another; they expressed them in suitable language, applied them to life-situations, and showed their perfect agreement with everything taught by right reason and philosophy, to which they added splendid new light. There is great scope in sacred doctrine for inventiveness which does not overstep the boundaries of the sacred deposit. St. Antoninus praises Aquinas for this very reason: 'He kept his reading and his methodology up-to-date, and offered new reasons for his conclusions.'*[44] And St. Augustine is impelled to say: 'The longer things lie hidden, the sweeter they are when found.'*[45] They did not exceed the limits of the deposit because they adhered to Tertullian's advice: 'Let us search in what is our own, and from our own people and what concerns our own; and for that only which, granted the rule of faith, can be questioned.'*[46] The part of doctrinal teaching drawn from their own understanding and spirit bestows upon the Fathers and other ecclesiastical writers variety of richness and style, but because style makes them progress in different, individual ways and modes they do not constitute at this level the same unshakeable authority proper to their unanimous witness of unique doctrine.

32. This is the explanatory unfolding of sound, unchangeable doctrine to which each particular intelligence can contribute according to its own God-bestowed gift. Vincent of Lerins, a 5th century Father, spoke about this unfolding in commenting on St. Paul's famous words to Timothy: 'Timothy, guard what has been entrusted to you. Avoid the profane innovations and contradictions of what is falsely called knowledge.'*[47] He first defines the deposit, asking: 'What is "The deposit"? That which has been entrusted to you, not that which you have yourself devised: a matter not of wit, but of learning; not of private adoption, but of public tradition; a matter brought to you, not put

[44] Part 3, Hist. tit. 23, c. 7.

[45] *Exposition on Psalm 106*, n. 14.

[46] *On the Praescription of Heretics*, c. 12.

[47] 1 Tim 6: 20.

forth by you, wherein you are bound to be not an author but a keeper, not a teacher but a disciple, not a leader but a follower.’*[48] Here lies the unity of doctrine. Then he goes on to consider how each doctrine is unfolded. He asks whether the inviolable unity of doctrine does not as a necessary consequence prevent any religious progress in the field of doctrine: ‘But perhaps some one will say. “Shall there, then, be no progress in Christ’s Church?”’*[49] He replies that progress, the unfolding of doctrine, is not only not lacking, but that it is endless, and the cause of concern amongst mankind which, in opposition to God, would prohibit it if possible: ‘Certainly; all possible progress. For what being is there, so envious of men, so full of hatred to God, who would seek to forbid it?’*[50]

Nevertheless, he wants this progress, described by him with great wisdom, not to detract in any way from the faith which progress is intended to help. ‘It must, however, be real progress, not alteration of the faith. For progress requires that the subject itself be enlarged, alteration requires that it be transformed into something else. The intelligence, then, the knowledge, the wisdom, as well of individuals as of all, as well of one man as of the whole Church, ought, in the course of ages and centuries, to increase and make much and vigorous progress; but yet only in its own kind; that is to say, in the same doctrine, in the same sense, and in the same meaning. The growth of religion in the soul must be analogous to the growth of the body, which, though in process of years is developed and attains its full size, yet remains still the same. There is a wide difference between the flower of youth and the maturity of age; yet they who were once young are still the same now that they have become old, inasmuch that though the stature and outward form of the individual are changed, yet his nature is one and the same, his person is one and the same. An infant’s limbs are small, a young man’s large, yet the infant and the young man are the same. Men when full grown have the same number of joints that they had when children; and if there be any to which more mature age has given birth these were already present in

48 [*Commentarium* 22, 4].

49 [*Ibid.*, 23, 1].

50 [*Ibid.*].

embryo, so that nothing new is produced in them when old which was not already latent in them when children. This, then, is undoubtedly the true and legitimate rule of progress, this the established and most beautiful order of growth, that mature age ever develops in the man those parts and forms which the wisdom of the Creator had already framed beforehand in the infant.'*[51]

33. We need to pay great attention to what this Father says about religion's continual advance through precious, new understanding not only on the part of the faithful, but also on that of the Church. The following words merit further explanation: 'The intelligence, then, the knowledge, the wisdom, as well of individuals as of all, as well of one man as of the whole Church, ought, in the course of ages and centuries, to increase and make much vigorous progress.'*[52] We can see how this is possible by looking at the history of the kingdom of God on earth.

34. Everything is preserved in the immobile deposit. But at the same time the Church defines single truths by means of new conciliar and dogmatic statements, or through papal bulls, and expresses them in precise canons. This occurs whenever it is clearly necessary or useful for the faithful, especially in the case of attacks and contradictions coming, under Providence, from the authors of different heresies and errors. Study, discussion and the writings of various Doctors and theologians prepare and formulate the canonical definitions which then become the fixed boundaries described by the Scriptures: 'Do not remove the ancient landmark that your ancestors set up.'*[53]

35. Moreover, the Church amplifies doctrine continually by means of new applications. Guided by the light of God, it focuses gospel morality on the new circumstances in which Christian society ceaselessly finds itself during its pilgrimage here on earth. The ample development of its disciplinary laws and of its magnificent worship serves the same purpose. This is the ecclesial progress and advance in understanding, knowledge and wisdom described by Vincent of Lerins, a successor in this

[51] [*Ibid.*, 23, 2–7].

[52] [*Ibid.*, 23, 4].

[53] Prov 22: 28.

matter to the holy Doctors and famous Fathers quoted by the Church herself in the great Councils.[54]

In his gospel, St. Luke says that Jesus 'increased in wisdom and in years, and in favour with God and man.'[55] The same can be said about the Church, made in the image and likeness of Christ. From a child, as she was in apostolic times, she has become an adult, developing in all her members, in her action, and in her self-presentation, as we can see with our own eyes after nineteen centuries of history. In her growth, the Church acts as Vincent describes: 'If there be anything which antiquity has left shapeless and rudimentary, [she intends] to fashion and polish it; if anything already reduced to shape and developed, to consolidate and strengthen it; if anything already ratified and defined, to keep and guard it. Finally, what other object have Councils ever aimed at in their decrees, than to provide that what was before believed in simplicity should in future be believed intelligently, that what was before preached coldly should in future be preached earnestly, that what was before practised negligently should thenceforward be practised with double solicitude?'*[56]

36. This is the only progress possible in the Church, the only increase to which dogma can be subject. According to Vincent of Lerins, progress comes about entirely on the level of forms and of evermore explicit declarations, which he describes as follows: 'In like manner, it behoves Christian doctrine to follow the same laws of progress, so as to be consolidated by years, enlarged by time, refined by age, and yet, withal, to continue incorrupt and unadulterated, complete and perfect in all the measurement of its parts, and, so to speak, in all its proper members and senses, admitting no change, no waste of its distinctive property, no variation in its limits.'*[57]

He goes on to speak of the studies and labour with which individuals amongst the faithful who possess the appropriate

[54] In the 5th Synod (or 6th, according to Gennadius): 'In all things we follow the holy men who were also holy teachers of the Church of God'* (p. 317). Many other Councils said the same.

[55] 2: 52.

[56] [*Commentarium* 23, 17–18].

[57] [*Ibid.*, 23, 9].

gift may cultivate the sacred deposit of faith. The doctrine of faith, he says, is like a grain of wheat growing until harvest, but without the admixture of cockle. He continues: 'This, rather, should be the result — there should be no discrepancy between the first and the last. From doctrine which was sown as wheat, we should reap, in the increase, doctrine of the same kind — wheat also; so that when in process of time any of the original seed is developed, and now flourishes under cultivation, no change may ensue in the character of the plant. There may supervene shape, form, variation in outward appearance, but the nature of each kind must remain the same. Therefore, whatever has been sown by the fidelity of the Fathers in this husbandry of God's Church, the same ought to be cultivated and taken care of by the industry of their children, the same ought to flourish and ripen, the same ought to advance and go forward to perfection. For it is right that those ancient doctrines of heavenly philosophy should, as time goes on, be cared for, smoothed, polished; but not that they should be changed, not that they should be maimed, not that they should be mutilated. They may receive proof, illustration, definiteness; but they must retain withal their completeness, their integrity, their characteristic properties.'*[58]

37. The matter could not be expressed more correctly nor precisely, and I shall have to limit myself to a comment on one of the many fine phrases in this passage. Vincent's *ut primis atque extremis sibimet non discrepantibus* [there should be no discrepancy between the first and the last] contains the rule for rightly amplifying sound doctrine and for judging where human intelligence may have departed from and betrayed it. Does a certain consequence follow by necessary inference from one or other of the revealed truths defined by the Church? If so, accept it unhesitatingly as a step forward. If it does not follow, or proves contrary to what is already known, reject it as erroneous and harmful. In this way, the 'principle of coherence' with what is revealed provides a clear path leading to the increase and unfolding of sacred doctrine. On the other hand, the 'principle of incoherence' is a sure criterion for discovering what is false and harmful in opinions suggested by fallacious reasoning.

[58] [*Ibid.*, 49–50].

Thus, the revealed truth remains one and the same; what harmonises with it does not divide it, because such a consequence is already present to it as the plant is implicitly contained in a seed.

Vincent encourages Christian teachers to study, and follow the footsteps of Bezalel by erecting with exquisite workmanship a spiritual tent of knowledge from the jewels and precious metals provided by divine revelation alone. Without adding anything substantially new, they are to burnish, sculpt and harmonise the whole with new, well-developed skills. 'O Timothy! O Priest! O Expositor! O Doctor! if the divine gift hath qualified you by wit, by skill, by learning, be a Bezaleel of the spiritual tabernacle, engrave the precious gems of divine doctrine, fit them in accurately, adorn them skilfully, add splendour, grace, beauty. Let that which formerly was believed, though imperfectly apprehended, as expounded by you be clearly understood. Let posterity welcome, understood through your exposition, what antiquity venerated without understanding. Yet teach still in the same truths which you have learnt, so that though you speak after a new fashion, what you speak may not be new.'*[59]

[59] [*Ibid.*, 22, 6].

CHAPTER 6

New and godless language compared with praiseworthy innovations first used by Christian teachers, and then by the Church herself

38. 'Test everything; hold fast to what is good', says St. Paul.[60] This is the discernment of spirit proper to Christianity which, co-terminous with truth and all that is good, embraces everything true and good. What we have said about doctrine, therefore, is also to be applied to the use of words: we have to distinguish between blameworthy and praiseworthy innovations.

In his first letter to Timothy, St. Paul puts him on his guard against the wrong kind of innovation, 'O Timothy, guard what has been entrusted to you. Avoid the profane innovations and contradictions of what is falsely called knowledge; by professing it some have missed the mark as regards the faith.'[61] He does not teach him to avoid all innovation in language, but *profane innovations* and *contradictions*, that is, everything opposed to the deposit of faith. He warns him against what is falsely called knowledge, the sole source of *contradictions*; he has no quarrel with true knowledge which can only be in complete agreement with the sacred deposit.

39. This was certainly the meaning given to Paul's splendid affirmation by ecclesiastical writers, including Fathers and Doctors of the Church. When St. Hilary admonishes Constantius with the words: 'The Apostle says that new, but profane language must be avoided. Why, therefore, do you exclude new, pious language?',*[62] he shows that he recognises the danger of godless innovation in language, but at the same time upholds holy, praiseworthy innovations which the Emperor, an Arian supporter, was not prepared to grant.

St. Thomas comments on the same passage from St. Paul:

[60] [1 Thess 5: 21].

[61] 1 Tim 6: [20–21].

[62] *Against the Emperor Constantius*, n. 16.

'Avoid profane innovations and contradictions': 'Not to want to hear anything new means barking against custom, but new, profane things are not to be heard. A profane innovation is present when something is said against the faith.'*[63]

In the preceding chapter we have shown that Catholic doctrine is susceptible of ever deeper investigation, but this would be impossible if language itself were unable to take on the new, richer expressions and modes contributed by all ecclesiastical writers. In his great work *On the Canonisation of Saints*,[64] Benedict XIV deals with the subject of praiseworthy, innovative language in his usual competent fashion, and offers several examples of the happy use of new words: 'purgatory', 'trinity of persons', 'incarnation', 'transubstantiation'. He cites other examples from work on the subject by Father Cajetan Benito de Lugo:[65] 'physical predetermination', 'middle knowledge', 'moral pre-motion', and 'effective, intrinsic assistance'. Similar expressions could be quoted endlessly from every school of Catholic theology. Fulgenzio Petrelli sums up the matter: 'There are two kinds of innovation, one commendable, the other detestable. It is detestable in so far as it is vain, useless, out of harmony with morality, contrary to the faith, opposed to the divine Scriptures, and attacks the holy Fathers. It is commendable in so far as it is serious, useful, true, constant, in harmony with morality, at one with the faith and Scripture, and with the Fathers.'*[66]

40. Innovative language is not only useful, but highly necessary in the face of sophisticated arguments from heretics accustomed to wriggling out of any situation in which they discover the slightest equivocation in expression. We need to note that language, especially the language of ordinary social life (and there is no other starting point) is poorly adapted for the precise expression of metaphysical concepts and sublime, theological doctrine. The same words often have several meanings, and can be employed in different ways by writers. An additional

[63] *Exposition on 1 Tim.*

[64] Bk. 2, c. 18, n. 6, 7.

[65] 'The prior, efficacious concursus of God necessarily coherent with human free will, free from necessity'* (*Disputation* 4, single paragraph).

[66] [*On the Beatification of the Servants of God*, etc., p. 275].

problem is the multiplicity of languages in which doctrines are expressed. If a person is not fully at home with them, they can be used improperly in writing or orally, or wrongly interpreted by the listener or reader. Nevertheless, none of these reasons caused damage to sound, Catholic teaching before the appearance of heresies. The Fathers were correctly understood even when they spoke with greater freedom[67] because the common faith was their interpreter. But those wishing to introduce errors against the faith quibbled over words and expressions used by the Fathers, taking their stand on the letter of what was written, which they used as an authority in their favour whenever they found it contained some ambiguity suitable for concealing the poison of their new, perverse teaching. At this point, defenders of the Catholic faith had to pin them down by discovering new expressions and definitions that rendered their deception impossible. This is the reason used by St. Augustine for justifying his own language and that of other Fathers in speaking about the blessed Trinity: 'We confess that these terms sprang from the necessity of speaking, when prolonged reasoning was required against the devices or errors of the heretics.'*[68]

Such praiseworthy and necessary innovation in expression, used in the first place by individual defenders of Catholic dogma, was often consecrated later by the authority of the Church in its canonical definitions: 'comprising a great amount of matter in a few words, and often, for the better understanding, designating an old article of the faith by some characteristic new name.'*[69]

[67] Cf. Petavius' observations on the Fathers' way of speaking in the first three centuries before the Arianism made its appearance (*The Trinity*, bk. 1, c. 1–3).

[68] *The Trinity*, 7, c. 4.

[69] *Commonitorium*, c. 23.

CHAPTER 7

Continuation. How heretics are and always have been enemies of praiseworthy innovation both in the development of the sacred deposit and in vocabulary

41. Heretics have always worn a mask of hypocrisy in their attempts to deceive the people and inject them with their own poison. They have paraded as enemies of innovation, accusing Catholic writers and teachers of scandalously novel opinions and expressions against which they appeal to venerated antiquity. But what has scandalised, and still scandalises them? They object to what we have described as natural, necessary, logical, praiseworthy innovations which in no way alter the deposit of faith. Without detracting from, adding to or altering the deposit, these innovations are intended to unfold it, illustrate it and preserve it unharmed. By applying the deposit to the varying circumstances of the Christian people, these writers unveil the immortal life of Christianity. But what is the real reason for the heretics' pretended devotion to antiquity? At stake is love of another kind of innovation: godless, execrable innovation that undercuts or caricatures the sacred deposit and, if heretics could succeed in their evil aim, would overthrow and supplant it.

Modern heretics disagree (do heretics ever agree?) about the precise period to which they should assign innovations in the life of the Church which, according to them, disguise or deprave the primitive teaching of Christ and the apostles. For many, this period coincides with the 4th/5th centuries; for others, with the 6th century, the century following, or even much later.

42. This is what we hear continually from Protestants, but heretics in earlier times adopted the same tactic. They took umbrage whenever the truths they wanted to overthrow were better explained or illustrated; they looked upon the praiseworthy innovations of holy teachers as godless innovations destined to challenge ancient doctrine. Arians accused St. Athanasius, and other defenders of the divinity of the

Word, of novelty; Pelagians charged St. Augustine in the same way.[70]

43. The accusation of innovation levelled against the Doctor of Grace has unfortunately been repeated innumerable times, even by presumptuous Catholic authors incapable of understanding the sublimity of the questions treated by Augustine. Although he has been effectively and repeatedly defended by learned theologians and by popes, this has not prevented obstinate, mediocre intellects from advancing the same slanderous denunciations. In effect, narrow, arrogant minds have unwittingly imitated heretical methods, parroting the few theological formulas they carry in their heads. One of the last heretics to attack St. Augustine for the impetus he gave to the development of Christian theology through the gift of intelligence bestowed upon him by God was the pseudo-Pherephonus who, in 1703, published at Antwerp or Amsterdam the *Animadversiones in S. Augustini Opera*. He was answered by the masterly Lamindo Pritanio.[71] But every holy Father or Doctor first illustrating some dogma and defending it against attack has been called an innovator. Catholic writers have always been accused in this way.

44. From the middle ages, before the birth of Scholasticism, it is sufficient to quote the example of St. Paschasius Radbertus, whose celebrated book *De Corpore et Sanguine Domini* was adopted as an authority by the Calvinists after they had altered and ruined it. As soon as the deception had been uncovered, and the book seen in its original, authentic text, it was bitterly contested by the Calvinists themselves as innovative. Many Catholics had indeed been frightened or taken off guard from the beginning by certain expressions in the work, as we shall see, although the Church found them wholly in keeping with

[70] St. Augustine, when accused by the Pelagians of adding something more precise to the language of preceding Fathers on the question of predestination, did not deny the charge but maintained that it was futile: 'What need is there, then, for us to look into the writings of those who, before this heresy sprang up, had no necessity to be conversant in a question so difficult of solution as this, which beyond a doubt they would have done if they had been compelled to answer such things?'* (*On the Predestination of the Saints*, c. 14).

[71] [Cf. Foreword, p. vii].

sacred tradition and well suited for expressing it with great precision.

The same kind of trick was used by heretics in accusing the Scholastics of innovation. As a recent theologian[72] has said, 'The Scholastics brought together the headings of Catholic doctrine, and in determining them by means of concise formulae followed teaching and tradition received in the Church. Thus they taught, amongst other things, that there are seven sacraments, that three of the sacraments impress the character, that the body of Christ is *really* and *substantially* present in the Eucharist; and they called *transubstantiation* the way in which Christ presents himself in the Eucharist.'[73] The Church then consecrated with its support these precise determinations of dogma offered by Scholasticism. Better established in this manner, dogma was protected from every danger of error and taught more easily to the people.

45. The Scholastics came under attack from Protestants especially, although Erasmus himself[74] and other 16th century humanists also criticised them. They were open to censure, of course, for their barbarous language and arid style, for their lack of critical sense, and for certain private opinions they expressed as individuals. These and other defects are fully recognised and noted by all the great Catholic theologians, for example Melchior Cani[75] and, in modern times, Bolgeni[76] who went too far in this respect. But the heretics' trick is to accuse the Scholastics in general of innovation, even in matters where their unanimity shows that they must be considered a link in the chain of Catholic tradition. Pius VI rightly suppressed and condemned certain theologians of the last [18th] century, dominated by *esprit de corps* and motivated by rashness rather than accuracy

[72] Perrone, [*Theological Lectures*], *De locis*, p. 2, sect. 2, c. 2, §7.

[73] The use of the words 'matter' and 'form' applied to the sacraments and accepted in the Council of Florence does not seem to go back further than William Antisiodorensis at the beginning of the 13th century. The expression *ex opere operato* was first used by Innocent III, and consecrated by the Council of Trent.

[74] Cf. Petavius, [*Dogmatic Theology*], *Proleg.*, c. 5, §6 and *ss.*

[75] [*Complete course of Theology*], *De locis theol.*, 8, 1.

[76] *Del possesso ecc.*

of doctrine, who assaulted Scholasticism itself, not the abuses of individual teachers, as if it had opened the floodgates to innovation. It will be useful to refer to the text of the Bull *Auctorem Fidei* which condemned the Synod of Pistoia: 'The accusation levelled against Scholasticism by the Synod (of Pistoia) maintained that "Scholasticism opened the way to new and self-contradictory systems relative to higher truths and finally led to probabilism and laxism." This accusation, in so far as it took no notice of individuals who could or did misuse Scholasticism, is false, rash, and injurious towards the holy men and teachers who brought great good to the Catholic religion through their study of Scholasticism. It also gives support to those who in heretical circles inveigh against Scholasticism.'*[77]

46. There is nothing more abhorrent to heretics than the natural, enlightened development brought about by the Church in the deposit of faith during the course of centuries. This development has ensured the continued identity of the deposit in the midst of new and ever more splendid expressions; it has gone hand in hand with the development of worship which, as part of Catholicism, has been able with its majestic splendour to attract, move and conquer heretics themselves, despite their prejudices. Amongst these heretics, some recognised the error in which they had been raised. Men of good will and able minds, although brought up on the false principle that every innovation in the Church is a deviation from primitive evangelical teaching, were able to reflect and see that the Church of Christ, which is not a corpse but a society living throughout the ages, possesses its own natural development as a consequence of its vital state. It was this thread of life which drew them along the way leading to entry into the Catholic Church. Two especially come to mind: Karl Ludwig von Haller who, despite his inborn prejudices, clearly recognised that the Christian religion is like a seed containing in itself the future tree (like the mustard seed that would develop throughout the ages), and embraced the truth without further difficulty, as he himself says in various places in his writings; and John Henry Newman who, on the basis of the natural development of Christian doctrine and practice, wrote the book that signalled his future conversion.

[77] [*Auctorem fidei*, 28].

47. The reason preventing heretics from tolerating the increasing light of truth that assures and illustrates the deposit of faith, and leading them to define it as 'novelty', also determines their hatred of the innovative language necessary for such development, and extremely useful in continually forming a more precise determination of the perpetual belief of the Catholic Church. Their attitude is formed by a desire to introduce surreptitiously, through captious interpretation of traditional or scriptural opinions, another kind of innovation relative to doctrine and expression, that is, the *profane innovation* condemned by St. Paul and abhorred by Catholics. The Fathers never ceased accusing heretics of such malicious inconsistency. St. Hilary reproved the emperor Constantius for refusing to accept the word *homoeusion* or *homoousion* because it was not found in the Scriptures, although the Emperor was ready to admit many other expressions not found there. It will be useful to read Hilary's own words which offer stringent reasons for proving the Church's power to adopt new formulae, and showing the utility and necessity for so doing. 'Amongst other things, he [Constantius] uses his cunning now as he did before to establish wicked things under the appearance of good, and crazy things as though they were reasonable. He says: "I do not want words which are not used in Scripture to be spoken." But let me put it to him, "What bishop orders this to be done? And which bishop forbids any form taken by apostolic preaching?".'*[78] Here Hilary shows that because the Church has been commissioned to preach the gospel, it has also received the power to establish the most opportune formulae for communicating and handing on the sacred deposit. He goes on to prove the necessity of new expressions and formulae. 'Tell me first, if you think this is rightly stated: "I do not want new medicines to fight new poisons; or new wars to fight new enemies; or new counsels to oppose new, insidious dangers." So, if the Arian heretics for the same reason avoid the word "homoeusion" (or "homoousion") today because they denied that it was used previously, are you going to run away from it today so that they also may deny it now? The Apostle tells us to avoid innovations in speech, but he is referring to profane innovations. Why, then,

[78] [Hilary of Poitiers, *Against the Emperior Constantius*, 16].

do you exclude pious innovations?'*[79] He then rebukes Constantius' inconsistency: 'You have never seen the word "unbornable" in writing, but do you reject it because it is new? The same can be said about "the Son is similar to the Father". The Gospels do not contain this word, but why do you reject it? Innovation is accepted in one case, but shied away from in another. Where impiety allows an opening, you allow innovation; where religion is extremely cautious, you exclude innovation.'*[80]

[79] [*Ibid.*, 594].
[80] [*Ibid.*].

CHAPTER 8

Continuation. The application and wisdom needed for avoiding and rejecting profane innovations in things and in words

48. The Catholic Church, taught and assisted by her divine Founder whose Spirit has formed her according to perfect freedom, knows that she has the power to teach the truth entrusted to her and to hand it on free from error without being tied in any material way to forms, opinions or words. When JESUS Christ sent the apostles to preach and to teach, he did not restrict their mission to any specific, determined mode, but left this to be suggested to his Church by the Spirit according to the needs of time and circumstances. 'But the Counsellor, the Holy Spirit, whom the Father will send in my name, he will teach you all things, and bring to your remembrance all that I have said to you'.[81] The Spirit that gives life to the Church teaches her all things. She cannot err because the Spirit moves her in whatever way she teaches these things, and he himself only suggests whatever she had first heard from JESUS Christ. The Church's freedom in her mode of teaching is a natural consequence of her unerring certainty; and the latter is a proof of the former.

49. JESUS Christ also said, 'Therefore I send you prophets and wise men and scribes.'*[82] These words clearly indicate the development his doctrine would undergo. On another occasion he had likened it to a grain of mustard seed that would grow to become the greatest of the shrubs. If instruction in revealed doctrine could be reduced to simple repetition of his divine words or those of the bible, without comment or development, there would be no need for him to send prophets, wise men and writers to his Church. It would have been sufficient to empower trustworthy mediocrities to repeat endlessly the formulae they had received. But St. Paul, one of the wise men and scribes promised by Christ, was conscious of his own particular mission, and that of others, when he wrote, 'God has made us

[81] Jn 14: 26.

[82] Matt 23: 34.

competent to be ministers of a new covenant, not in a written code but in the Spirit; for the written code kills, but the Spirit gives life.'*[83] Moreover, the Spirit of Christ guides not only teachers in the Church, but listeners also, so that they may understand what is said. Consequently St. Paul's other words, recommending in thought and life the Christian freedom given by Christ through his Spirit, are applicable to all things, 'Now we are discharged from the law, dead to that which held us captive, so that we may serve not under the old written code, but in the new life of the Spirit.'*[84]

50. The same divine Spirit who assures both the Church and the private teacher accepting the Church as master and teacher that the received truth will not be falsified by the way in which it is expressed, also inspires the Church and her followers with horror and detestation for godless innovations in fact and vocabulary. The Fathers and ecclesiastical writers, who are at one about this, go further by indicating which matters are godless innovations, and which are not.

Detestation, horror and discernment of godless truths are the fruit of the Spirit, and can never be lacking in the Church and amongst holy people. On occasion, such abhorrence is expressed by means of the holy, fiery zeal with which the Church expels heretics, and individual teachers attack them with irrefutable arguments drawn from the Scriptures or tradition or reason itself.

[83] 2 Cor 3: 6.

[84] Rom 7: 6. Cf. *About the Author's Studies (Introduction to Philosophy*, vol. 1, Durham, 2004): on Christian freedom of thought.

CHAPTER 9

Zeal against heretical waywardness has to be combined with knowledge and discretion if errors of judgment are to be avoided

51. The faithful, however, have to combine zeal with discretion and knowledge if they are to avoid St. Paul's admonishment, 'I bear them witness that they have a zeal for God, but it is not enlightened.'*[85] Holy zeal coming from God is not to be confused with defects arising from human weakness. Pure zeal has to be free from every rash judgment involving doctrine and persons. It has to be directed against recognised and sure evil, without doing harm to what is good, or ignorantly judging what is good as though it were bad. I am not speaking of latter-day Pharisees who under cover of burning zeal directed at godless innovations air their own malice or secret passion, or even insinuate error. My target rather is the defect found in eager, half-educated, impetuous souls who easily become the involuntary instruments of the Pharisees mentioned above. The same defect is present in others whose lack of clear vision, while making them hesitant and uncertain in their judgments, gives them a strong distaste for every kind of controversy, which they look upon as out of place. They are afraid of disturbing charity, as though someone willing to maintain charity could do so by sacrificing the truth.

These over-delicate, perpetual fence-sitters have caused as much trouble to wise men in the history of the Church as that inflicted upon them by malicious persons. The attempt by the wise to throw more light on the most difficult questions has led to accusations of error or at least of imprudence, despite the approval given by the Church to wise teachers whose doctrines she has praised.

52. Amongst the down-hearted at the time of St. Augustine were those wearied by the arguments about the question of the dogma of predestination, and overcome by its difficulty. For them, it would have been better if Augustine had never spoken

[85] Rom 10: 2.

about it: 'They were so disturbed by what he was saying and so affected by weariness that the meaning of predestination, which he was constantly and urgently preaching, would, they thought, be better not mentioned. It seemed either on the verge of falsity or, as it were, extremely dangerous.'*[86] It is true that the arguments occasioned by the teaching of St. Augustine were endless, but finally, to the great embarrassment of his adversaries, the Catholic Church precluded all dissent by the canons of the 2nd Council of Orange which, accepted by the whole Church, attained the authority of an ecumenical council. These canons were composed of Augustine's own words. The Roman church also declared on several occasions that her teaching on grace and free will was the same as Augustine's much maligned doctrine.[87]

53. The history of sacred theology is full of similar examples, one of which will be sufficient to illustrate the rest. St. Paschasius Radbertus, whom we have mentioned above, threw new light on the doctrine of the holy Eucharist. His famous book *On the Lord's Body and Blood* was simply a faithful exposition of the doctrine of the Church about the Eucharist, but the precision of its formulas gave it an air of novelty, and caused a good deal of hesitation amongst contemporary Catholic teachers who had not sufficiently examined the argument. To some, it seemed that Paschasius had given more force to expressions used by Jesus Christ than they did in fact possess;[88] others found their faith undermined through not recognising their own beliefs in the expressions employed by Paschasius (Frudegard, to whom the saint wrote a long letter, seems to have been amongst these); finally, Paschasius' book gave others the opportunity of raising a question that had long remained unclear: was

[86] c. 35 [Remigius of Lyons, *Liber de tribus epist.*].

[87] St. Hormisdas' statement on the matter in his letter to Possessor is one amongst many, and will suffice here: 'What the Roman, that is, the Catholic Church, follows and preserves about free will and the grace of God can be discovered in various books of blessed Augustine, especially those written to Hilary and Prosper, etc...'*

[88] He himself affirms this in his *Commentaries on St. Matthew*: 'I have said this more at length and expressly because I have heard that some take me up as though in that book which I wrote about the sacraments of Christ I had wanted to give more force to these words than the Truth himself did.'*

the body of Christ the same as that touched and seen (in a word, did it act in a physical way on our sensory organs), or was the body and blood of Christ only present under the veil of the species of bread and wine?

What had the holy Abbot done? Remaining faithful to the doctrine of the Church, he had tried to make the teaching clearer and easier to understand for the children of Saxon converts at school in the monastery of Corbie. He says: 'Although I wrote nothing in this book worthy of its readers (I dedicated it to youngsters), nevertheless I hear that it has helped many to an understanding of this mystery, enabling them to think worthily of Christ...'*[89] St. Odo of Cluny witnesses to the value of the work in illustrating the mystery when he says that Paschasius had written it in accordance with the opinions of the Fathers 'in order to enhance reverence towards the holy mystery and reveal its majesty. If anyone reads it, even an educated person, I believe he will learn as much about this mystery as he thinks he already knows.'*[90] This is the kind of explanation of dogmas and mysteries that we have already spoken of; it is the aim of Catholic theologians and teachers as they strive to add understanding to their study of the faith. Noël Alexandre made the same point in his learned defence of Paschasius against the accusation of innovation brought against him by the Calvinists. He affirms that the understanding of the mystery of the Eucharist encouraged by Paschasius amongst so many of the faithful is not confined to the ordinary knowledge brought by faith and needed for salvation, but is a kind of enlightened, excellent knowledge which takes account of the circumstances of the mysteries, analogy with the prophets of the Old Testament, the purpose, the effects and benefits, and the dispositions needed in order to take part in them.'*[91] Alexandre continues his comment on what I may call the learned knowledge of the dogmas of faith, saying: 'This knowledge is called "understanding" by St. Augustine also. It does not precede, but follows faith as a reward. "So accept, so believe", he says in sermon 51 on the words of the Lord, "that

[89] *Letter to Frudegard.*

[90] *Conferences*, bk. 2, c. 30, 31.

[91] *Ecclesiastical History*, 9th and 10th Centuries, Diss. 10, §4.

you may be rewarded with understanding. For faith must precede understanding if understanding is to be the reward of faith".'*[92]

54. Notwithstanding the clarity with which Paschasius had expounded the Church's doctrine on the sacrament of the holy Eucharist, he became the unsuspecting occasion of argument, censure and hesitant faith. His clarity, in fact, served to fuel the dispute. Those who felt they were fully instructed, but were ignorant of what Paschasius taught about the great mystery, thought that his teaching was an innovation incompatible with the doctrine of faith, because their belief lacked the intellectual light with which his books enhanced it. This light blinded the unsuspected weakness of their own eyes. They grumbled in secret and even their faith suffered, although they dared not contradict him openly. Paschasius knew very well that their errors were the result of their ignorance: 'and so although it is ignorance which leads them to err in this matter, no one is prepared to come out into the open and contradict that which the whole world believes and confesses.'*[93] A little later he calls them: 'Chatterboxes rather than learned,'*[94] although this does not prevent him from instructing them and trying to show them where they were wrong.

55. The Church gained two special advantages from the discussions stimulated by Paschasius' book, both of which are of great importance. First, many questions were clarified which previously had not been treated in depth; in addition, as a consequence of the first advantage, more precise language was discovered and determined in relationship to the Eucharist. This language, in harmony with the expressions used by Radbertus, was then sanctioned by the Church.

In his book, and in his letter to Frudegard, Paschasius had said that the Eucharist was simultaneously *truth* and *figure*. Rathmanus, a monk of the same monastery of Corbie, who had written a book on the Eucharist at the command of Charles the Bald, accepted the real presence, but took the word *truth* for *manifestation*, the meaning which, according to him, Gregory

[92] *Ibid.*

[93] *Letter to Fredugard.*

[94] *Ibid.*

had given it.[95] As a result, he denied that Christ was present in truth in the Eucharist, and asserted that he was there only in mystery or in figure, that is, covered by the veil of the species. This teaching differed only in expression from that of Paschasius; but it was a substantial question relative to those who erroneously thought that Christ himself was perceptible to the senses in the eucharistic bread and wine. Rathmanus did not distance himself from Catholic dogma, but the expression he used, taken out of its context, was open to equivocation.

56. In his historical preface to Rathmanus' book, Jacques Boileau, a Parisian theologian (1712), shows how the monk had been accused of heresy, even by very learned persons, and his work placed on the list of prohibited books; later he was proclaimed the precursor of Calvinism by Arduin in a dissertation on the subject. Boileau goes on in his appendix to the book to show how Rathmanus had finally been fully justified and proved free of every suspicion of heresy.*[96] This defence of Rathmanus has been recognised as solid by later historians of theology.

Rathmanus himself offers a twofold example of the ease with which people too sure of their own judgment can deceive themselves when they lack depth of doctrine and neglect to examine a subject carefully before accusing writers, who otherwise are wholly Catholic, of godless and dangerous innovations. On the one hand, Rathmanus is an example of this in his opposition to Paschasius, if indeed it is true that he intended to attack Radbertus' book in his own work of the same name, *De Corpore et Sanguine Domini*, as Erigerus claims in a book commonly attributed to the anonymous Cellotian; on the other hand, Rathmanus himself has been accused of heresy by learned men throughout the ages.

57. St. Paschasius' book gave rise to another question. He had

[95] The words used by Gregory are: 'Lord, may your sacraments perfect in us what they contain, so that what we do now in *specie*, we may receive in *rerum veritate*.'* These words have been misused by many heretics. But they refer to what we perceive of the sacrament, not to the sacrament itself, and they ask that the Christ whom we now receive under the species, that is, contained in the sacred sign, we may one day receive without veil or mystery.

[96] [Jacob Boileau, *Dissertation on the book* 'The Lord's Body and Blood'].

affirmed that in the holy Eucharist the flesh of our Saviour was 'without doubt that which was born of Mary, and suffered on the cross, and rose from the tomb.'*[97] St. Ambrose had already given his support to this way of speaking.[98] Nothing, in fact, could be more Catholic. But at the time such a precise expression appeared an unusual innovation, not only amongst the uneducated, but even to the learned. Rabanus Maurus, for example, the famous bishop of Magonza, opposed it. He had discovered that St. Augustine and St. Jerome had spoken as though three bodies of the Lord could be distinguished, the Church, the Eucharist, and that born of the Virgin. He accused Paschasius of not having taken care to reconcile St. Ambrose with the statements of the other two Fathers. Mabillon shows that Rabanus' affirmation did not depart from Catholic doctrine of the real presence. He did not deny that the body of Christ in the Eucharist is identical *naturaliter*, that is, really and substantially, with the body born of the Virgin Mary and crucified, but only *specialiter*, that is, according to species and outward form.[99] It has to be admitted that this is idle subtlety, because the identity or non-identity of the body does not lie in the external species, but in its substantial union with the soul. In this sense, Paschasius' way of speaking is absolutely true, and later accepted universally by theologians. Nevertheless, Rabanus censured it, as Rabanus himself later encountered unmerited censure.

58. I could have given many other examples of controversies arising from writers' expounding with greater conceptual clarity and verbal precision the Catholic dogma they wished to illustrate. The clarity was new, and the precision unusual, to many who had not examined their faith to the same degree. Accustomed to less exact language and somewhat indeterminate concepts, they were nevertheless convinced that their knowledge was sufficient and their belief fully enlightened.

[97] [*On the Lord's Body and Blood*].

[98] *On the Mysteries*, c. 9.

[99] Mabillon, Preface to Part 2 of 4th century [*Acta Sanctorum ordinis Benedictini in saeculorum classes distributa*] where again he justifies Rabanus against another accusation, that is, that the body of Christ, when received by a communicant, undergoes the same changes as other foods.

Disputes arose, and accusations of error were brought against people who least deserved them. But from all this God drew advantage for his Church; the truth surfaced, and shone more brilliantly as a result.

CHAPTER 10

The theological and logical rules to be followed in judging the waywardness or soundness of a Catholic writer

59. As long as the Church has not passed judgment on the waywardness or soundness of the teaching of a Catholic writer, private theologians must abstain from inconsiderate censure of the author, although there is nothing to prevent their offering to the public a balanced and objective opinion. For a theological judgment to be true, it must be proposed by a person who follows certain logical and theological rules, in addition to those required by courtesy and charity. These norms have been the object of much learned discussion, and in their wisest expression have been followed by Roman censorship, and sanctioned or explained by Benedict XIV in his Bull *Sollicita* or in his *De Canonisatione Sanctorum*. We need not go into them in detail, therefore, but confine our examination to the fundamental principle, found in the Fathers of the Church, governing a theological judgment. Afterwards, we can add the four rules suggested for ecclesiastical censors by Lamindo Pritanio in his book, *De Ingeniorum Moderatione*, quoted often by Benedict XIV.

The principle to be kept in mind by theologians undertaking to censure an author arises as a corollary of the relationship of Christian freedom to points of doctrine. As we have said, Christ did not tie his teaching to determined forms or words, but simply entrusted the deposit of his doctrine to the Church. He left it to be unfolded and announced in every tongue and in every possible form of language, style and eloquence, on condition that it remained identical and entire, without the addition of any really new item, or the loss or omission of any other.

This holy, splendid freedom left by Christ to the reverent understanding of those believing in his word gives rise to the following corollary: as Christian doctrine is not to be found only in the words it employs, but in the sense contained in the words, so too error and heresy does not consist in the words or forms used, but in what they mean. The Fathers and ecclesiastical writers are all fully agreed about this.

60. St. Hilary points to this truth when he shows that holy Scripture is not found in its material phrases, but in the understanding of the doctrine they contain. Heretics can read the written words, but they do not penetrate to the doctrine: 'Scripture has to be understood, not simply read.'*[100] Jerome says the same: 'Scripture has to be understood, not simply read. Otherwise, if we follow the letter, we ourselves could make up new dogma.'*[101] St. Augustine also observes that heretics do not despise the letter of Scripture in their possession; their error consists in not possessing the doctrine contained in the letter: 'They are heretics not because they despise what the Scriptures contain, but because they do not understand them.'*[102] Finally, St. Athanasius observes that as far as possible heretics conceal their errors under the very words of Scripture: 'The devil, the author of heresies, because of the ill savour which attaches to evil, borrows Scripture language as a cloak wherewith to sow the ground with his own poison also, and to seduce the simple.'*[103]

These examples show that it is not sufficient for an author to use Catholic phrases or words, and other uncensurable expressions, in order to forestall criticism. His work has to be examined at greater depth, and the whole of his arguments taken into consideration. Only the entire context will show whether the argument contains unsound doctrine. Cicero expresses this rule of logic when he says of philosophers: 'They are not to be considered on the basis of their vocabulary, but by reason of their perspicacity and constancy.'*[104]

61. But if this principle can be validly employed to uncover error hidden in a sheath of words, it must also be used with respectful care for recognising the truth in Catholic writers, and in all devout writing, even that inspired by God. Hence St. Hilary can add (and this is another part of the same principle): 'Heresy is about understanding, not about written words. We are

[100] *Against the Emperor Constantius*, 2, 9.

[101] *Dialogue against the Luciferarians.*

[102] *Letter 120*, n. 13.

[103] *Against the Arians*, Orat. 2.

[104] *Tusc.*, 5, 4.

dealing with wilfully mistaken meaning, not with speech.'*[105] St. Ambrose agrees: 'The letter is not mistaken; no fault is to be found in the written word; it is the meaning which is at fault.'*[106] And St Hilary synthesises the two parts of the principle: 'The understanding of what is said is to be found in the cause of what is said. What we talk about is not to be subject to the word, but the word to what we talk about.'*[107] The 'cause of what is said' is to be understood as the author's entire purpose, which is demonstrated through his complete context, his accurate comparison with parallel passages, his definitions of words, and by means of every indication provided by hermeneutics and sound criticism.

In principle, therefore, it is the teaching which merits approval or censure, not its forms and words unless they prejudice the teaching or conceal error, or alter the truth through poor exposition.

62. We can now set out the four rules suggested by Lamindo Pritanio in the book we mentioned.

The first rule. 'Ecclesiastical censors do indeed have to take suitable precautions about every innovation in opinions and terminology, but not in such a way that they immediately judge as new everything which seems new to them. Nor should they imagine that what really is new is to be condemned out of hand because it is new.'*[108]

The author adds the following comment to the first rule. He first shows how the theological censor has to be cautious, and careful not to permit in the books he censures any godless innovation that may depart in the least from Catholic dogma. But he also insists on the necessity of sound doctrine in the censor. Without it, ignorance could easily lead him to abuse the first rule: 'Note, however, that ignorance can easily abuse this rule. Everything seems new to the unlearned, who were previously ignorant of what they are now reading. It would be ridiculous, and a sin against justice if, because of their ignorance, they want to reject these things, or overlay them with suspicion. It is obviously harmful that the studies of learned men should be hidden

[105] *The Trinity*, 4, 9.

[106] *On the Faith*.

[107] *The Trinity*, bk 4, 14.

[108] *On moderating able people in religious matters*, 2, 6.

away because they do not suit the palates of certain people. Censors and judges, rather than silence the learned, should take care to investigate whether these things are both new and dangerous.'*[109]

63. *The second rule*. 'A prudent person does not tolerate books and discourses which can give rise to scandal; but it is equally true that a prudent person should not suppress the power that intelligent people and writers have of tracking down error and superstition and thus preventing these evils from flowing without hindrance throughout the Church.'*[110]

Here, the learned writer shows that authors are not to be tolerated who reprove abuses so discourteously, imprudently and boastfully that they cause people to hate and despise the holiest things. On the other hand, he also shows that those uncovering and attacking abuses zealously, knowledgeably and prudently have to be granted a certain freedom in their war on matters that, within ecclesiastical circles, can cause great damage to the kingdom of God on earth: 'When this is done modestly and prudently, no one will begrudge such necessary medicine to the Church. But why do you so easily forbid publication to their writings, or insist that they be withdrawn from the public? False accusations of impiety are made against practically all the ancient works of the holy Fathers. Indeed, we can read in their works such sharp discourses against corrupt clerics and monastic customs, against superstitious and pious practices, and against licence in opinions and vices in prelates that we would not want to repeat them. But no scandal resulted, and no one censored them. We have become so delicate that we cannot tolerate the slightest disturbance, and are always afraid of the evil pressing on us from without.'*[111]

64. *The third rule*: 'A prudent person tries to weigh all things carefully so that he may, as far as possible, condemn the error or cause of error in books. But the prudent person, who wishes to act cautiously in these matters, also takes note of the scruples, quibbling and acerbity which he may find in himself.'*[112]

[109] [*Ibid.*].

[110] [*Ibid.*].

[111] [*Ibid.*].

[112] [*Ibid.*].

65. In this rule the author praises careful censors who reject error, and everything else that could cause error or vice, but he expects this laudable attention to be free from three defects: scruples, quibbling and acerbity. In order to avoid misunderstanding, he goes on to describe each of them in detail. First, scruples: 'For me, scruples consist in suspecting heresy on all sides, and in constant fear that heresy may inflict damage on religion, or that contempt and hatred be caused towards our venerated predecessors or against sacred things, or that readers be faced with error to the detriment of their morals.'*[113]

Then quibbling: 'For me, quibbling consists in always wanting to accept in the worst way whatever seems to offer an easy, solid meaning and to lead most conveniently to an explanation consonant with upright, correct faith.'*[114]

Finally, acerbity: 'Acerbity means having the kind of spirit that wishes to place obstacles to the publication of books, or suppress those works which can easily be amended. Or the spirit that wishes, out of misplaced sincerity towards holy Church, to deal totally inflexibly with authors, to deter them from writing and frequently to undermine their work and good name without sufficient cause. These authors do no harm to the Church or to readers however strongly, sharply and freely they write. Writing and distributing books of this kind is of great assistance to the well-being of peoples and the Church.'*[115]

66. *The fourth rule* for balanced censorship: 'A prudent person tries, as far as possible, to keep at a distance things which may cause harm, provided he does not deprive the Church or the State of a remedy greater than the danger, or block some greater utility.'*[116] The author illustrates this rule with several examples, one of which I shall quote. He insists that if history were compelled to be silent about the errors and public vices of rulers, even of our ecclesiastical rulers, the prohibition would do the Church and public affairs more damage than good. But criticism has to be offered without rancour, from love of what is true and good, and with courteous reverence and charity: 'If the

[113] [*Ibid.*].

[114] [*Ibid.*].

[115] [*Ibid.*].

[116] [*Ibid.*].

faults the writer points to are true, and anger or denigration are not the author's motive, freedom of this kind and care for the truth are sometimes to be tolerated. Moreover, senior people in the Church, and ecclesiastics of any kind, should be reminded that their own good name is at stake. This will act as a brake on their asking what is impossible and on other sordid vices proper to worldly people.'*[117] After affirming that many of the Church's highest dignitaries were unfortunately subject to these vices, he adds: 'If we are going to write about what these people did, is it lawful to describe them as other than they were? Is their good name to be boosted by adulation?'*[118] And he makes the following objection: 'But these things are to be passed over, you say. Yes, I would agree, if they are faults of a private person and are guiltless relative to the people and religion; if nothing useful is served by their revelation, and even more if revelation could harm the State; and again, if these guilty persons are still alive. If, however, the crimes are public and connected with religious and ecclesial business, and their dead perpetrators have been placed in the pillory, it would perhaps be more useful for the benefit of the State if these human vices were brought to light rather than dissimulated. Vice will exist as long as there are human beings, but it should be accused and disapproved and its horror impressed upon human beings lest it roam about unpunished. Those who come after will learn from the example of their predecessors what is to be done. They will also learn respect for their own good name if, while respecting the living, they treat all the dead equally, and acknowledge the baseness they express under quite different appearances. It is sometimes useful to the Church and the State that these things should be made known.'*[119] He supports his case with the example of Baronius, a free, impartial historian.

I have quoted these long passages from this learned, devout and illustrious writer because I could never have expressed myself so ably and with such holy zeal. Moreover, his authority gives greater weight to teaching that harmonises so well with the common sense of theologians and of mankind in general.

[117] [*Ibid.*].

[118] [*Ibid.*].

[119] [*Ibid.*].

Original Latin References

The numbers are footnote numbers

3. *Vel rei magnitudine, vel doctoris imperitia, vel audientis duritia.*

4. *Sumite materiam vestris, qui scribitis, aequam viribus; et versate diu quid ferre recusent, quid valeant humeri.*

5. *Brevis esse laboro, obscurus fio.*

7. *Haereticos malo suo veris Catholicis Christi membris prodesse, dum Deus utitur et malis bene et diligentibus Deum omnia cooperantur in bonum.*

8. *Ad exercendas et elimandas quodammodo mentes legentium, et ad rumpenda fastidia atque acuenda studia discere volentium, celandos quoque sive ut ad pietatem convertantur, sive ut a mysteriis secludantur, animos impiorum.*

12. *Qui ea quae pro natura quaestionum dilucide dicta existimo, adhuc non intellegunt, non mihi calumnientur pro neglegentia vel pro meae facultatis indigentia, sed Deum potius pro accipienda intellegentia deprecentur.*

13. *Prorsus intellegor, velis, nolis; sed tu nihil contra ista dicturus, vis non intellegi quod ego verissimum atque firmissimum dixi.*

14. *Quod difficilius quaeritur solet dulcius inveniri.*

15. *Mundum tradidit disputationi eorum, ut non inveniat homo opus, quod operatus est Deus ab initio usque ad finem.*

16. *Quia ista scientia est principaliter de his quae sua altitudine rationem transcendunt.*

17. *Verbi Dei altitudo exercet studium, non denegat*

intellectum. Si enim omnia clausa essent, nihil esset unde revelarentur obscura. Rursus, si omnia tecta essent, non esset unde alimentum perciperet anima et haberet vires quibus posset ad clausa pulsare.

19. *Attende tibi et doctrinae, attende lectioni, exhortationi et doctrinae.*

21. *Vide prius utrum ista petitio cum tua superiore definitione concordet.*

22. *Neque enim cum coepero te in tanti huius secreti intellegentiam utcumque introducere (quod nisi Deus intus adiuverit, omnino non potero) aliud disserendo facturus sum, quam rationem, ut potero, redditurus.*

23. *Quam si a me, vel a quolibet doctore non inrationabiliter flagitas, ut quod credis intellegas, corrige definitionem tuam, non ut fidem respuas sed ut ea, quae fidei firmitate iam tenes, etiam rationis luce conspicias.*

24. *Absit namque, dice, ut hoc in nobis Deus oderit, in quo nos reliquis animantibus excellentiores creavit. Absit, inquam, ut ideo credamus, ne rationem accipiamus sive quaeramus; cum etiam credere non possemus, nisi rationales animas haberemus.*

25. *Porro autem qui vera ratione iam quod tantummodo credebat intellegit, profecto praeponendus est ei qui cupit adhuc intellegere quod credit; si autem nec cupit, et ea quae intellegenda sunt, credenda tantummodo existimat, cui rei fides prosit, ignorat: nam pia fides sine spe et sine caritate esse non vult. Sic igitur homo fidelis debet credere quod nondum videt, ut visionem et speret et amet.*

26. *Anima itaque considerata, maxime humana et rationalis atque intellectualis, quae et eius imaginem facta est, si cogitationes nostras et intellegentias non evicerit, sed eius quod habet praecipuum, id est ipsam mentem atque intellegentiam mente atque intellegentia potuerimus adprehendere, non erit fortassis absurdum, ut eam ad suum quoque Creatorem intellegendum, ipso adiuvante, meditemur adtollere. Si autem in seipsa deficit, sibique*

succumbit, pia fide contenta sit, quamdiu peregrinatur a Domino, donec fiat in homine quod promissum est, faciente illo 'qui potens est' sicut ait Apostolus 'facere supra quam petimus et intellegimus'.

27. *Ipsumque lumen, quo cuncta ista discernimus, in quo nobis satis apparet quid credamus incognitum quid cognitum teneamus, quam formam corporis recordemur, quam cogitatione fingamus, quid corporis sensus adtingat, quid imagineatur animus simile corpori, quid certum et omnium corporum dissimillimum intellegentia contempletur: hoc ergo lumen, ubi haec cuncta diiudicantur, non utique sicut huius solis et cuiusque corporei luminis fulgor per localia spatia circumquaque diffunditur, mentemque nostram quasi visibili candore illustrat, sed invisibiliter et ineffabiliter, et tamen intellegibiliter lucet, tamque nobis certum est, quam nobis effecit certa quae secundum ipsum cuncta conspicimus.*

28. *Quo cuncta ista discernimus.*

29. *Ubi haec cuncta diiudicantur.*

30. *Tamque nobis certum est, quam nobis efficit certa, quae secundum ipsum cuncta conspicimus.*

31. *Accipere potest* [*sacra doctrina*] *aliquid a philosophicis disciplinis, non quod ex necessitate eis indulgeat, sed ad majorem manifestationem eorum quae in hac scientia traduntur.*

32. *Sed propter intellectus nostri: qui ex his, quae ad naturalem rationem (ex qua procedunt aliae scientiae) cognoscuntur, facilius manuducitur in ea, quae sunt supra rationem.*

35. *In lectionibus Apostolicis superioribus, quas charitati vestrae, quantum Dominus adiuvare dignatus est, exposuimus, multum laborem et sollicitudinem passi sumus. Compatiebamur vobis et solliciti eramus et pro nobis et pro vobis. Quantum autem existimo adiuvit Dominius et nos et vos; et ea quae prorsus difficillima videbantur sic per nos enodare dignatus est, ut nulla quaestio remaneret, quae conturbet mentem piam. Impia enim mens odit etiam ipsum intellectum.*

36. *Sunt enim quaedam quae vi sua non intelleguntur, aut vix intelleguntur, quantolibet et quantumlibet, quamvis planissime, dicentis versentur eloquio; quae in populi audientiam, vel raro, si aliquid urget, vel numquam omnino mittenda sunt. In libris autem qui ita scribuntur ut ipsi sibi quodam modo lectorem teneant cum intelleguntur, cum autem non intelleguntur, molesti non sint nolentibus legere, et in aliquorum conlocutionibus non est hoc officium deserendum, ut vera, quamvis ad intellegendum difficillima, quae ipsi iam percepimus, cum quantocumque labore disputationis ad aliorum intellegentiam perducamus, si tenet auditorem vel conlocutorem discendi cupiditas nec mentis capacitas desit, quae quoquo modo intimata possit accipere: non curante illo, qui docet, quanta eloquentia doceat, sed quanta evidentia.*

38. *Non opus fuisse huiuscemodi disputationis incerto, minus intelligentium tot corda turbari; quoniam non minus utiliter sine hac definitione praedestinationis per tot annos defensa est Catholica fide.*

39. *Augustini doctrina de praedestinatione plurimos ex fidelibus, praesertim ex iis qui in Gallia morabantur, non solum indoctos sed etiam doctos, mirum in modum turbavit, ne dicam illius occasione salutem eorum fuisse periclitantem.*

40. *Qui ea quae pro natura quaestionum dilucide dicta existimo, adhuc non intellegunt non mihi calumnientur pro neglegentia, vel pro meae facultatis indigentia, sed Deum potius pro accipienda intellegentia deprecentur.*

41. *Recensito autem hoc Beatitudinis tuae libro (De correptione et gratia), sicut qui sanctam atque apostolicam doctrinae tuae auctoritatem antea sequebantur, intellegentiores multo instructioresque sunt facti, ita qui persuasionis suae impediebantur obscuro, aversiores quam fuerant recesserunt.*

42. *Nec tanta perturbatione et permotione fidelium, ab intentione veracissimae et fidelissimae doctrinae suae frangi potuit, aut revocari; sed magis eos et scriptis suis inquantum potuit admonuit et instruxit, et orationibus apud Deum profusis fideliter adiuvit, ut intelligerent et agnoscerent*

quam necessario et quam salubriter propter commendationem divinae gratiae eiusdem preaedestinationis veritas omnino et credenda et praedicanda esset.

44. *Erat enim in legendo novos articulos adinveniens, novumque modum determinandi inveniens et novas producens in determinationibus rationes.*

45. *Quam dulciter inventa, quae diu latentia.*

46. *Quaeramus ergo in nostro et a nostris et de nostro; idque dumtaxat, quod, salva regula fidei potest in quaestionem devenire.*

47. *O Timothee, depositum custodi, devitans prophanas vocum novitates.*

48. *Quid est depositum? Id est quod tibi creditum est, non quod a te inventum; quod accepisti, non quod excogitasti; rem non ingenii sed doctrinae; non usurpationis privatae sed publicae traditionis; rem ad te perductam, non a te prolatam; in qua non auctor debes esse, sed custos; non institutor sed sectator; non ducens sed sequens.*

49. *Sed forsitan dicet aliquis: nullusne in Ecclesia Christi profectus habebitur religionis?*

50. *Habeatur plane et maximus. Nam quis ille est tam invidus hominibus et exosus Deo, qui istud prohibere conetur?*

51. *Sed ita tamen ut vere profectus sit ille fidei, non permutatio. Siquidem ad profectum pertinet ut in semetipsum unaquaeque res amplificetur; ad permutationem vero, ut aliquid ex alio in aliud transvertatur. Crescat igitur oportet et multum vehementerque proficiat tam singulorum quam omnium, tam unius hominis quam totius Ecclesiae aetatum ac saeculorum gradibus, intellegentia, scientia, sapientia, sed in suo dumtaxat genere, in eodem scilicet dogmate, eodem sensu eademque sententia. Imitetur animarum religio rationem corporum: quae licet annorum processu numeros suos evolvant et explicent, eadem tamen quae erant permanent. Multum interest inter pueritiae florem et senectutis maturitatem: sed iidem tamen ipsi fiunt senes, qui fuerant adolescentes: ut quamvis unius eiusdemque hominis status*

habitusque mutetur, una tamen nihilominus eademque natura, una eademque persona sit. Parva lactentium membra, magna iuvenum; eadem ipsa sunt tamen. Quot parvulorum artus tot virorum; et si qua illa sunt quae aevi maturioris aetate pariuntur, iam in seminis ratione proserta sunt; ut nihil novum postea proferatur in sensibus quod non in pueris iam ante latitaverit. Unde non dubium est hanc esse legitimam et rectam proficiendi regulam, hunc ratum atque pulcherrimum crescendi ordinem, si eas semper in grandioribus partes ac formas numerus detexat aetatis, quas in parvulis Creatoris sapientia praeformaverat.

52. *Crescat igitur oportet et multum vehementerque proficiat tam singulorum quam omnium, tam unius hominis quam totius Ecclesiae aetatum ac saeculorum gradibus intelligentia, scientia, sapientia.*

53. *Ne transgrediaris terminos antiquos, quos posuerunt patres tui.*

54. *In omnibus sequimur et sanctos et doctores sanctos Dei Ecclesiae.*

56. *Omni industria hoc unum studet ut vetera fideliter sapienterque tractando, si qua sunt illa antiquitus informata et inchoata, accuret et poliat; si qua iam expressa et enucleata consolidet, firmet; si qua iam confirmata et definita, custodiat. Denique quid unquam aliud conciliorum decretis enisa est nisi ut, quod antea impliciter credebatur, hoc idem postea diligentius crederetur; quod antea lentius praedicabatur, hoc idem postea instantius praedicaretur; quod antea securius colebatur, hoc idem postea sollicitius excoleretur?*

57. *Ita etiam Christianae religionis dogma sequatur has decet profectuum leges, ut annis scilicet consolidetur, dilatetur tempore, sublimetur aetate, incorruptum tamen illibatumque permaneat, et universis partium suarum mensuris, cunctisque quasi membris ac sensibus propriis plenum atque perfectum sit quod nihil praeterea permutationis admittat nulla proprietatis dispendia, nullam definitionis sustineat varietatem.*

58. *Quin potius hoc rectum et consequens est ut, primis atque extremis sibimet non discrepantibus, de incrementis triticeae institutionis triticei quoque dogmatis frugem demetamus; ut cum aliquid ex illis seminum primordiis accessu temporis evolvatur, et nunc laetetur et excolatur, nihil tamen de germinis proprietate mutetur. Addatur licet species, forma, distinctio, eadem tamen cuiusque generis natura permaneat... Quodcumque igitur in hac Ecclesiae Dei agricultura fide patrum satum est, hoc idem filiorum industria decet excolatur et observetur, hoc idem floreat et maturescat, hoc idem proficiat et perficiatur. Fas est enim ut prisca illa caelestis philosophiae dogmata processu temporis excurentur, limentur, poliantur; sed nefas est ut commutentur, nefas ut detruncentur, ut mutilentur. Accipiant, licet, evidentiam, lucem, distinctionem; sed retineant necesse est plenitudinem, integritatem, proprietatem.*

59. *O Timothee, o sacerdos o tractator o doctor, si te divinum munus idoneum fecerit, ingenio, exercitatione, doctrina, esto spiritalis tabernaculi Beseleel; praetiosas divini dogmatis gemmas exculpe, fideliter coapta, adorna sapienter, adiice splendorem, gratiam, venustatem. Intellegatur, te exponente, inlustrius quod antea obscurius credebatur. Per te posteritas intellectum gratuletur, quod ante vetustas non intellectum venerabatur. Eadem tamen quae didicisti, doce, ut cum dicas nove, non dicas nova.*

62. *Novitates vocum, sed profanas devitare jubet Apostolus: tu cur pias excludis?*

63. *Devitans profanas vocum novitates, quia non velle audire aliquid novi est oblatrare contra consuetudines; sed nova prophana non sunt audienda. Sed prophana novitas est, quando inducitur aliquid contra fidem.*

65. *Concursus Dei praevius et efficax neccessario cohaerens cum libero arbitrio a neccessitate libero.*

66. *Novitas duplex esse potest, alia commendabilis, alia detestabilis. Detestabilis est, quae vana, inutilia, falsa moribus, fidei contraria, pugnantia cum Scripturis divinis, sanctisque patribus pronuntiat. Commendabilis vero est,*

quae seria, utilia, vera, constantia, veris consona, moribus appositia, fidei convenientia, sacris paginis, et patribus refert.

68. *Fatemur loquendi necessitate parta haec vocabula, cum opus esset copiosa disputatione adversus insidias vel errores haereticorum.*

69. *Magnam rerum summam paucis litteris comprehendendo, et plerumque propter intelligentiae lucem, non novem fidei sensum, novae appellationis proprietate signanda.*

70. *Quid igitur opus est, ut eorum scrutemur opuscula, quia priusquam ista haeresis oriretur, non habuerant necessitatem in hac difficili ad solvendam quaestionem versari? Quod procul dubio facerent, si respondere talibus cogerentur.*

77. *Insectatio, qua Synodus (Pystoriensis) Scholasticam exagitat, velut eam 'quae viam aperuit inveniendis novis, et inter se discordantibus systematibus, quoad veritates maioris pretii, ac demum adduxit ad probabilismum et laxismum'; quatenus in Scholasticam reiicit privatorum vitia, qui abuti ea potuerunt, aut abusi sunt: falsa, temeraria, in sanctissimos viros, et doctores, qui magno Catholicae religionis bono scholasticam excoluere, iniuriosa, favens infestis in eam haereticorum conviciis.*

78. *Utitur autem etiam nunc in caeteris ante, artis suae consuetudine, ut per recti speciem prava confirmet, et per rationis nomen insana constituat. 'Nolo,' inquit, 'verba quae non scripta sunt dici.' Hoc tandem rogo: 'Quis Episcopus iubeat? Et quis apostolicae praedicationis vetet formam?'*

79. *Dic prius, si recte dici putas: Nolo adversum nova venena novas medicamentorum comparationes; nolo adversum novos hostes, nova bella; nolo adversum novas insidias, consilia recentia. Si enim Ariani haeretici idcirco homoeusion (al. homousion) hodie evitant quia prius negaverunt; nonne tu hodie idcirco refugis, ut hi nunc quoque denegent? Novitates vocum, sed profanas devitare jubet Apostolus: tu cur pias excludis?*

80. *'Innascibilem' scriptum nusquam legis: numquid ex hoc*

negandum erit, quia novum est? Decernis 'similem Patri Filium'. Evangelia non praedicant: quid est quod refugis hanc vocem? In uno novitas eligitur, in alio submovetur. Ubi impietatis occasio patet, novitas admittitur: ubi autem religionis maxima et sola cautela est, excluditur.

82. *Ecce ego mitto ad vos prophetas at sapientes et scribas.*

83. *Idoneos nos fecit ministros novi testamenti, non littera sed spiritu: littera enim occidit, spiritus autem vivificat.*

84. *Soluti sumus a lege morttis, in qua detinebamur, ita ut serviamus in novitate spiritus et non in vetustate litterae.*

85. *Testimonium perhibeo illis quod aemulationem Dei habent, sed non secundum scientiam.*

86. *In tantum permoti fuerunt, et quodam taedio affecti, ut praedestinationis sensum, qui ab eo constanter et instanter praedicabatur, vel quasi falsum, vel quasi valde pericolosum potius tacendum judicarent.*

87. *De arbitrio tamen libero et gratia Dei quid Romana, hoc est Catholica, sequatur et servet Ecclesia, licet et in variis libris beati Augustini, et maxime ad Hilarium et Properum, possit cognosci etc..*

88. *Haec idcirco prolixius dixerim et expressius, quia audivi quosdam me reprehendere quasi ego in libro, quem de Sacramentis edideram Christi, aliquid his dictis plus tribuere voluerim, quam ipsa Veritas repromittit.*

89. *Quia etsi nil in eo legentibus dignum scripsi, quem cuilibet puero dedicavi, tamen ad intelligentiam huius mysterii plures, ut audio, commovi... ut sciant et intelligant digne cogitare de Christo.*

90. *...ad reverentiam sancti mysterii commendandam atque majestatem ejus demonstrandam. Quae si quis, licet sciolus legerit, tanta credo discet, ut de hoc mysterio parum se eatenus cognovisse putet.*

91. *Sed luminosam quamdam et excellentem notitiam, quae mysteriorum cirumstantias, analogiam ad prophetias*

Veteris Testamenti, finem, effectus, fructusque, ac dispositiones ad illorum participationes adhibendas assequitur.

92. *Quam notitiam intelligentiae nomine sanctus etiam Augustinus significat, quae fidem non praecedit, sed sequitur ut merces: sic accipite, inquit sermone 51 de Verbis Domini, sic credite ut mereamini intelligere. Fides enim debet praecedere intellectum, ut intellectus fidei sit praemium.*

93. *Et ideo quamvis ex hoc quidem de ignorantia errent, nemo tamen est adhuc in aperto, qui hoc ita esse contradicat, quod totus orbis credit et confitetur.*

94. *Loquacissimi magis quam docti.*

95. *Perficiant in nobis tua, Domine, Sacramenta quod continent, ut quae nunc specie gerimus, rerum veritate capiamus.*

96. *Contra Joannem Harduinum S. J. presbyterum, ab omni novitatis aut haeresis calvinianae suspicione et inventione vindicatur.*

97. *Non aliam plane quam nata est de Maria, et passa in cruce, et resurrexit de sepulchro.*

100. *Scripturae enim non in legendo sunt, sed in intelligendo.*

101. *Scripturae non in legendo consistunt, sed in intelligendo; alioqui si litteram sequimur, possumus et nos quoque novum nobis dogma componere.*

102. *Ac per hoc non quod eas contemnant, sed quod eas non intelligant, haeretici sunt.*

103. *Excogitator inventorque haereseon diabolus, metu suae graviolentiae Scripturarum voces usurpat, ut illis obtectus, aspersus veneno suo simplices decipiat.*

104. *Non igitur ex singulis vocibus philosophi spectandi sunt, sed ex perspicuitate atque constantia.*

105. *De intelligentia enim haeresis, non de Scriptura est, et sensus, non sermo fit crimen.*

106. *Littera errorem non habet, apices sine crimine sunt, sensus in crimine.*

107. Intelligentia enim dictorum ex causis est assumenda dicendi, quia non sermoni res, sed rei est sermo subjectus.

108. Censores Ecclesiastici sibi metuere debent ab omni novitate sententiarum atque verborum, sed ita tamen ut ne quidquid novum sibi videtur, continuo tale iudicent, aut quidquid novum revera est damnandum quoque illico arbitrentur.

109. Sed animadvertendum facile ignorantiam abuti posse hac lege. Indoctis nova omnia videntur, quae illa antea ignorarunt. Quid, si velint haec ideo repellere, aut erroris suspicione onerare? Hercle id ridicule fiat, et in iustitiam peccetur. Quis moleste non ferat, eruditorum hominum studia latere et iacere debere, quod peregrinum sapiant quorumdam palato? Ad Censores potius ac Iudices pertinet diligenter investigare, an ea nova sint, simulque perniciosa, quam ad eruditos silere.

110. Prudentis quidem est libros et orationes non tolerare, e quibus scandala exoriri possint: sed aeque prudentis est, ita ingeniis atque scriptoribus non adimere potestatem insectandi erroris atque superstitionis, ut haec mala per Ecclesiam sine obice fluere et bacchari exinde pergant.

111. Quum id modeste prudenterque peragitur, quid invides Ecclesiae necessariam utilemque medicinam? Cur tam facile eorum scriptis lucem negas, aut eripis? Omnia fere Sanctorum Patrum, et antiquorum volumina aliquas habent falsae pietatis accusationes. Immo acerrimae apud illos leguntur orationes, quales ne imitari quidem prorsus nos vellemus in corruptos clericorum et monachorum mores, in superstitiosas parumque pias consuetudines, in licentiam opinionum et vitia praesulum. Nulla inde tamen scandala consequuta sunt, et illis nemo succenset. Nos adeo delicati evasimus ut ne leves quidem puncturas ferre possimus, atque extranea inde semper mala timeamus.

112. Prudentis est, caute omnia perpendere ut quantum potest, errorem aut errorum, atque vitiorum caussam in libris damnet. Sed a prudentia discedit qui tam caute agere vult, ut in scrupulos postea et cavillationes et asperitatem nimiam se proripi non animadvertat.

113. *Scrupulos appello, ubique haereses suspicari, ubique metuere, ne religioni vulnera infligantur, ne in venerandos maiores, atque in sacra contemptus aut odium creetur, neve lectoribus propinentur errores, eorumque moribus officiatur.*

114. *Cavillationes voco in deteriorem partem accipere semper velle, quae sanum facile pariunt sensum; et sive sententiae, sive sint voces, explicationem rectae fidei ac honestati consonam commodissime admittunt.*

115. *Asperitates nomine significare animus est, tot obices interdum opponere editioni librorum, aut quae facile emendari possunt, prorsus opprimere velle; aut scriptores, Ecclesiae sanctae ob sinceritatem, quam profitentur nimum necessarios, rigidissime semper excipere, eorum calamos deterrere, eorum labores ac famam levibus nonnumquam de caussis divexare. Neque enim quaecumque fortia, acria, et magna cum libertate scribuntur, Ecclesiae nocent, sive lectoribus. Huiusmodi quoque libros conscribi interdum atque vulgari, plurimum conducit profecto populorum atque Ecclesiae regimini.*

116. *Prudentis est ita depellere, quae nocere possunt, ut interim tamen remedium ipsum maiorem non adferat Ecclesiae atque Reipublicae perniciem, aut maiorem non impediat utilitatem.*

117. *Quod si crimina vera memoriae produntur, neque livor, neque obtrectatio calamum scriptoris abripiunt, interdum toleranda erit huiusmodi libertas et veritatis cura. Oportet enim, timorem quoque famae instare principibus in Ecclesia viris, et ecclesiasticis quibusve, quo etiam freno coerceantur tum ab impotentia dominandi, tum a reliquis sordidissimis saecularium hominum vitiis.*

118. *Si horum gesta literis consignanda sunt, num alios homines describere licet, quam ipsi fuerunt? Num adulatione, fama eorum palpanda?*

119. *At ista, inquies dissimulanda. Utique, si crimina privati hominis sint; si nihil rei cum populo et Religione habeant; si nihil utilitatis, eoque magis si quidquam incommodi in*

Rempublicam fluere potest ex eorum revelatione; si denique a vivis nondum excessere criminosi. Verum cum pubblica sint scelera, et cum Religionis atque Ecclesiae negotio coniuncta sunt, eorumque auctores humanis rebus defuncti, irae atque vindictae locum sustulere: videndum est, an non maiorem Respublica utilitatem capiat, iisdem proditis, quam dissimulatis hominum vitiis. Erunt vitia, donec homines; sed ne vitia impunita debacchentur, arguenda sunt atque improbanda palam, eorumque horror incutiendus hominibus. Ex maiorum autem exemplis discunt successores, quid sibi agendum non sit; discunt vereri famam, parcentem quandoque viventibus, in mortuos omnes aequam, agnoscunt turpitudinem suam, aliena sub imagine expressam. Interest igitur Ecclesiae atque Reipublicae ista quoque interdum vulgari.

Index of Biblical References

Numbers in italic indicate the footnote number. Bible references are from RSV (Common Bible)

Index of Persons

Numbers in roman indicate paragraphs; numbers in italic indicate footnotes

General Index

Numbers in roman indicate paragraphs; numbers in italic indicate footnotes